Navajo Motif *by Joanne Mattera. A linen warp is combined with a wool weft in this piece.*

Pillow *by Joanne Mattera. This large wool pillow was worked in the simple angle tapestry technique.*

Rectangle *by Joanne Mattera. Simple stripes and rectangles combine in this wool hanging.*

Pyramid Piece *by Joanne Mattera (Left). This geometric hanging was worked with both a wool warp and weft.*

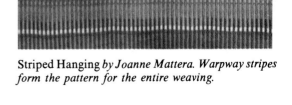

Striped Hanging *by Joanne Mattera. Warpway stripes form the pattern for the entire weaving.*

Untitled Hanging *by Joanne Mattera. This piece, woven on a floor loom, uses tapestry techniques such as interlocking and the simple angle.*

TO CHRISTIE—
HOPING YOU WILL SPEND
MANY LONG YEARS
MAKING FINE
OBJETS DE ART— KS

398

3/4

NAVAJO TECHNIQUES FOR TODAY'S WEAVER

NAVAJO TECHNIQUES FOR TODAY'S WEAVER

BY JOANNE MATTERA

WATSON-GUPTILL PUBLICATIONS, NEW YORK

PITMAN PUBLISHING, LONDON

First published 1975 in the United States and Canada by Watson-Guptill Publications,
a division of Billboard Publications, Inc.,
1515 Broadway, New York, N.Y. 10036

Library of Congress Cataloging in Publications Data
Mattera, Joanne, 1948-
    Navajo techniques for today's weaver.
    Bibliography: p.
    Includes index.
    1. Hand weaving. 2. Indians of North America—
Textile industry and fabrics. 3. Navajo Indians
Industries. I. Title.
TT848.M38   746-1′4   75-12648
ISBN 0-8230-3153-5

Published in Great Britain by Sir Isaac Pitman & Sons Ltd.
39 Parker Street, London WC2B 5PB
ISBN 0-273-00094-2

Manufactured in U.S.A.

First Printing, 1975
Second Printing, 1977

To my sisters everywhere

CONTENTS

Acknowledgments   8
Introduction   9

1. A NAVAJO HISTORY   11

Plain Stripe Blankets   12
Woman's Dress   13
The Bayeta Serape   14
The Chief's Blanket   14
Bosque Redondo   15
The Chief's Blanket   16
Moki and Banded Blankets   18
The Late Serape Style   19
The End of the Classic Period   20
The Boom or Transition Period   20
Eye Dazzlers   20
The Outline Style   21
Pictorial Weaving   22
The Yei Blanket   23
The Rug Period   24
The Revival Period   24
Contemporary Weaving   24

2. WEAVING MATERIALS   29

Shearing   29
Carding   31
Spinning   32
Color   33
Bayeta   33
Yarns   35
What Is Used Today   35

3. MAKING THE LOOM   37

Materials   39
The Frame   39
The Movable Loom   39
The Warping Frame   42
The Warp   43
Twining   45
Binding the Warp on to New Dowels   46
Setting the Warp Into the Frame   48
Making the Sheds   50

4. USING THE LOOM 53

Weaving 53
Weaving Particulars 58

5. WEAVING TECHNIQUES 61

Fine Horizonal Stripes 64
Beading 65
Alternating Blocks 66
Slit Tapestry 67
Comb Pattern 68
Interlocking 69
Dovetailing 70
Angles 71
Dovetailed and Serrated Angles 72
The Lazy Line 73
The Wedge Weave 74
Weaving the Design 76
The Whipped Edge 78
Finishing 79
Other Techniques 79

6. LOOM VARIATIONS 83

Lumber 83
A Word about Dowels 84
Hardware and Tools 85
Loom Frame Variations 88
Substituting Materials 86
Making a Heddle Rod Holder 96
Making the Loom Stationary 98
Substituting for the Forks and Batten 101
Finishing 103

7. WARPS AND YARNS 105

The Warp 105
Warping Variations 106
Heddle Variations 108
Yarns and Fibers 109
Carrying the Weft Through the Shed 111
Project Suggestions 113

8. OTHER TECHNIQUES 115

Twining 115
Two Colors on One Shuttle 117
Ghiordes Knots 118
Making a Curved Line In Weaving 118
Weaving the Circle 120
Tapestry Method 121
Slit Tapestry 123
Dovetailing 124
Feathering 125
Brocading 126
Ghiordes Knots 127
Project Suggestions 129

9. SOLVING PROBLEMS 131

Running Out of Warp Thread 131
Uneven Tension 133
Uneven Spaces Between Warp Threads 134
Poor Shed 134
Edges Pulling In 134
Uneven Selvedge 136
Straightening a Row 136
Broken Warp Threads 137
Weft Floats 138
Warp Showing Through the Weft 139

10. FINISHING 141

Pressing and Blocking 141
Overhand Knot 142
Braiding and Wrapping 143
Folded and Hemmed Edge 144
Warp Ends Pulled Into the Weft 145
Adding Fringe 145
Weaving the Edge 146
Hanging 147

Glossary 153
Suppliers List 155
Bibliography 157
Index 158

ACKNOWLEDGMENTS

Much energy from many different sources went into the production of this book. I would like to thank my parents for their long-standing and continuous support; Sally and Ray Waitkins for their encouragement and advice at the inception of this project; the women of the Green Mountain Weavers Guild in Bennigton, Vermont and the Arachne Women of Albany, New York, for their ideas and beautiful woven pieces; Linda Wager, Pam Scola, and George Schaub for developing my photographs; my students, my friends, and my dear sisters for their never-ending interest and support; and finally, Jennifer Place and Diane Hines, my editors, who put this book together. Thank you.

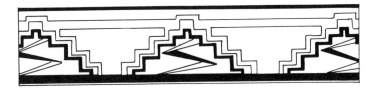

INTRODUCTION

I am not a Navajo weaver, and I assume that you, reader, are not either. We do not come from a culture where weaving is learned early, where working with the wool is a time-honored and traditional occupation, and where all women have the opportunity to work as artists within the society. There is a high level of quality in the great majority of Navajo weavings; it seems as if the command of design and color comes as easily as breathing (or weaving). Amazingly, preliminary drawings are rarely made, except when a weaver is duplicating a piece or creating a custom order. This indicates a consistently high degree of vision and technical expertise.

Obviously for me to tell you how to make an "authentic" Navajo blanket or rug, or for you to attempt it, would be folly. But the loom and the weaving techniques are very adaptable, and that is one reason why Navajo weaving persists today. I suggest that you work *with* the adaptability of the tools and the medium. Bring your experiences, color and design sense, reverence for the materials, and innovative ideas to your weaving, and in this way make Navajo weaving techniques work for you.

The first part of this book will cover the history and techniques of traditional Navajo weaving. The rest of the book contains variations and adaptions of, and additions to, the traditional techniques and materials. It offers you a glimpse at how some contemporary weavers are working with inspiration from the Navajo culture.

Except where otherwise noted, all photographs and illustrations are by the author.

A Variety of Rugs. *Photo by Ray Manley.*

A NAVAJO HISTORY

Certain historical events in the lives of the Navajo Indians, and consequently the weavers, make it impossible to divorce the history and stylistic development of the woven blanket from its historical context. So, while this chapter is not a history of the Navajo people, the history certainly must be considered. On that note let us look at the groundwork that was laid for the emergence of Navajo weaving.

At least 800 years ago, possibly more, the Navajo Indian tribes migrated from Northwestern Canada to northwestern New Mexico. Little is known about the culture that far back; oral legends and myths may exist but we do not know them. The fact is that the written history of the Navajos began when white men became interested in their land.

The Dînéh, the "People of the Earth," were semi-nomadic farmers and hunters. The hunters of the Dînéh augmented their supplies by raiding Pueblo, Mexican, and Spanish settlements to the south. It was in this way that they began to acquire sheep. The Navajos had been at odds with the Pueblo Indians for centuries and as the Spanish introduced sheep to the Pueblos, the Navajo flocks increased. Perhaps the hunters learned that it was easier to procure meat this way than by chasing antelope and deer. In any case, the large flocks of sheep tended by the Navajo were their meat source, and the life of the shepherd fit in well with their already semi-nomadic existence.

When the Pueblo rebellion against Spanish rule occurred in 1680, many Pueblos not involved in the fighting moved on to Navajo lands to escape retaliation from Spanish authorities. A number of Pueblos, refugees from their own land, intermarried and merged into the Navajo tribes. Other Pueblos maintained their identity, but after several years the close relationship fostered the exchange of ideas and skills.

The Pueblos were weavers, and it is most likely that they shared this knowledge with the Navajos. Interestingly, it was the Pueblo males who taught the Navajo females how to weave, and the tradition for both groups has scarcely changed since. More interesting still is the fact that from ancient times the material for Pueblo weaving was cotton, while the Navajo women seem to have started immediately with wool. The Navajos gained a large number of sheep as a result of the Pueblo revolt, and it seems a natural development for them to have spun the fleece and woven on looms made according to Pueblo specifications.

By the beginning of the 18th century, the Navajo women

were weaving. As the years went on, many types of woven goods were produced, among them the woman's dress and the saddle blanket. But it was the wearing blanket that was the popular trade item, and that is the focal point of this chapter.

The function of the wearing blanket was to keep the wearer warm. Yet the definition of "blanket" goes well beyond the limited concept that we now have of the word. Primarily the blanket was worn as a garment. Draped over the shoulders, it either hung down covering the arms or was pulled across the body. It was worn lengthwise in the case of the serape blanket and widthwise with the chief's blanket.

If you examine any blanket, you will see that what appears as top and bottom in any serape blanket, or as sides in the chief's blanket, actually meet at the front of the wearer. These two "half" designs unite to form a design that duplicates the whole figure at the back. This mode of wearing makes the blanket visually forceful. In the words of Mary Kahlenberg and Anthony Berlant, it is "as if each blanket were a diagram of the spiritual presence of an individual." (*The Navajo Blanket*, p.28.) This total effect should not be confused with the specific designs in the woven piece, however, for they had no spiritual significance at all.

The blanket was also used for bedding, and when hung in the doorway of the hogan to keep out the cold, the blanket was seen in much the same way as we see blankets today—as art on a two-dimensional surface.

PLAIN STRIPE BLANKETS

The earliest blankets, those woven between 1700 and 1800, were designed in the Pueblo tradition with alternating bands of natural colors. These designs may have been simple, but the weaving was of such high quality that by the end of the 1700's the supremacy of Navajo weaving was acknowledged; the Navajo women were established as weavers, and their weaving was established as industry. Trade began with other Indians and with the Spanish.

The colors of these first blankets were natural colors of the sheep: white, brown/black and grays made from combining the two. The yarn, of course, was hand-spun. Occasionally blue or red yarns were added sparingly. The blue dye, indigo, was obtained from the Spanish in blocks or chunks of solid coloring matter and then used to dye the natural white yarn. The red threads came from the unraveled bayeta cloth imported by the Spanish from England.

This early weaving only exists today as fragments gathered primarily from the Cañon del Muerte, Massacre Cave, where the Spanish clashed with the Navajos over warrior raids on Spanish territory. The examples were preserved only because the cave is relatively inaccessible.

Although the plain stripe blanket is known to have been the style woven almost exclusively throughout the 18th century, it was in fact woven well into the 19th century. So only a general chronology can be set up as a guide to its stylistic development.

The plain stripe blanket gave way to two distinctive weaving styles: the bayeta serape and the chief pattern blanket. The two styles developed simultaneously. It is important to remember

Plain Stripe Blanket. *The Museum of the American Indian, New York. Heye Foundation.*

the the location of the weavers throughout the territory, the availability of particular materials, and the skill and personal design preference of the individual weaver had a great deal to do with the two styles developing concurrently.

WOMAN'S DRESS

Before leaving the early stages of weaving, I would like to mention the woman's dress. In a society where the importance of women was acknowledged, and where women were the weavers, it is logical to assume that some of the first products of the loom would be items woven for themselves. The woman's dress was made from two identically woven pieces of fabric that were sewn together at the shoulders and down the sides, with ample room left for the neck and armholes. Because the dress was used only by the members of the tribe that wove it, the style never changed radically from its simple design. At the outset the dress was woven with the main body in brown/black or gray with stripes of other natural yarns at the bottom and top. Later the body became indigo blue with touches of bayeta red.

The dress is a modification of a style learned early from the Pueblos, and a comparison with the Pueblo woman's dress will bear this out. The style existed for almost 150 years until commercially made clothing was introduced in the middle of the 19th century.

Woman's Dress and Blanket, *c. 1850. The Field Museum of Natural History, Chicago.*

Bayeta Serape-Blanket. *The Field Museum of Natural History, Chicago.*

Poncho Blanket. *The Museum of the American Indian, New York. Heye Foundation.*

THE BAYETA SERAPE

The bayeta serape or blanket gets its name from the small amount of bayeta flannel used in it. Bayeta was a woolen flannel cloth woven in England, imported by the Spanish to the Pueblos, and obtained by the Navajos either by trade or devious means. The yardage was unraveled, and the fine woolen threads were rewoven into the blanket in either single or multiple strands. The primary reason for this tedious and time-consuming operation was the fine red color of the thread.

The serape is basically a rectangle almost twice as long as it is wide. When a slit was woven into the center of the serape it became a garment similar to the Mexican poncho. If you recall how the blanket was worn, you will realize that the poncho style, worn over the head and hanging on the shoulders, would necessitate somewhat different design considerations.

The bayeta serape or blanket started simply enough with small diamond or cross motifs on a plain stripe background. The early bayeta blankets were predominantly white and brown/black, with a little bayeta red and perhaps indigo blue. Occasionally bayeta green or yellow was used. The value of the blankets increased in proportion to the amount of bayeta used, and the amount of bayeta increased as the style developed.

The style became more complex and more Spanish in feeling, probably because it was a special trade item to the Spanish, who regarded the bayeta blanket with the highest esteem. The style reached near perfection in color, design, and quality in the sixty-three years of its existence. It stopped abruptly in 1863, when the Navajo people were rounded up and incarcerated at Bosque Redondo. Bayeta cloth was no longer available, and the Navajo people were enduring the worst years of their history.

THE CHIEF'S BLANKET

Before I talk about what effect this ordeal at Bosque Redondo had on the people and their weaving, let me take you through two phases of the chief's blanket, since that style paralleled the existence of the bayeta blanket.

The word "chief" is misleading, since the blanket could be worn by any male of the tribe. (The women wove a style for themselves called simply the woman's blanket, which was smaller and plainer since they also wore the woven dress.) It is possible that since it was a popular trade item, the blanket was worn by chiefs of other tribes and from that use received its name.

Although the chief's blanket existed contemporaneously with the bayeta blanket, its style was an ultimate simplicity rather than the controlled complexity of the bayeta designs. Interestingly, this style is the only one in which the width of the blanket is greater than the length; the blanket is approximately a third again wider than it is long. Such dimensions indicate a Pueblo influence.

The style is separated into several phases of design growth. The earliest chief blankets consist of even horizontal bands of alternating white and brown/black with narrower stripes of bayeta red, indigo blue, and in rare cases a bayeta or native-dyed green.

The second phase essentially follows the same format, but inserted within the striped field are narrow rectangles. This was the first break in selvedge to selvedge weaving in the style. As in the first phase, there is no background or foreground but rather a contained, balanced energy.

Bosque Redondo

Between 1600 and the mid-1800's the Southwest was in a state of flux. Spanish rule was constantly being challenged by both Mexicans and Indians; treaties were made and broken; Indians clashed with one another. White men were heading westward, anxious to gain a foothold in the territory. The Navajo warriors were able to use this time to their advantage; their raids were conducted with less risk and more profit. But this also proved to be their undoing.

Chief's Blanket, *2nd phase. The Museum of the American Indian, New York. Heye Foundation.*

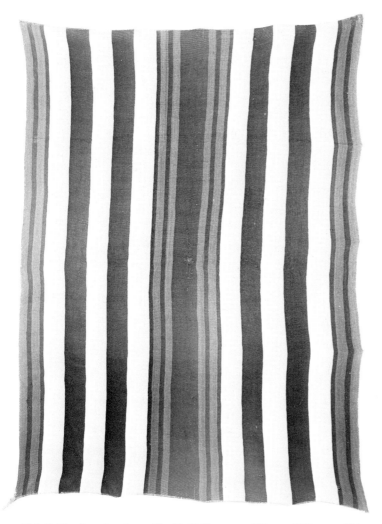

Chief's Blanket, *1st phase. The Field Museum of Natural History, Chicago.*

By the time the United States took control of Santa Fe (and consequently the greater Southwest) from the Spanish in 1846, the reputation of the Navajo warriors was as bad as that of the weavers was good. Peace treaties were established between the U.S. government and various Navajo tribes. But because the Navajo did not act as a unified whole, tribes that did not sign felt no need to honor those treaties. Consequently the government mistakenly saw the Navajos as untrustworthy, and they began their plans to wipe them out.

In 1863, aided by the Pueblos and the Ute who were anxious to retreive some of their lost livestock, Kit Carson and his soldiers burned Navajo homes and crops. It seems to have been a relatively bloodless coup. Yet faced with a decimated homeland and with the winter upon them, most Navajos surrendered to the government when promised rations. Marched 300 miles to Fort Sumner in east central New Mexico, 7,000 surviving Navajos were forced to live on an arid 40 acres under government coercion to become farmers.

It is small wonder that weaving almost stopped. Yet there were some strong and brave women who despite almost no available wood or materials built their looms and continued to weave.

The Navajo weavers were now exposed to white culture. Soldiers oftentimes supplied the weavers with materials in return for "souvenir" blankets, but how much of that weaving was voluntary is hard to say.

For five years the Navajos continued to live in poverty, oppressed and under white male domination. Finally, in 1868, they signed a peace treaty with the government that allowed them to return to their homeland if they promised to refrain from raiding Mexicans, other Indians, and the incoming whites.

The Navajos began to replant and to build up a flock of sheep. With so few sheep at the outset of this rebuilding period, and consequently so little wool, the weavers were ready for the onslaught of commercial materials that would steadily grow throughout the next decade.

THE CHIEF'S BLANKET, TRANSITIONARY AND THIRD PHASES

After Bosque Redondo, the chief's blanket evolved through a transitionary and then a third phase. In the transitionary period, triangular or diamond forms began to emerge from the rectangles of the second phase. By the third phase, the stepped-edge diamond became the center motif, with quarter and half diamonds placed equally around it in the corners and along the sides. In all there are nine figures.

The purest form of the phase occurs when the stripe and diamond appear as a balanced composition and neither motif takes precedence—an emergence of the serape and early chief designs. In many blankets of this period, the diamonds push to the foreground and begin to develop along the lines of the late serape style.

Chief's Blanket, *3rd phase. Collection of Rick and Judy Martell, Hoosick, New York.*

Chief and Serape Style Blanket *(fragment). The Field Museum of Natural History, Chicago.*

MOKI AND BANDED BLANKETS

Moki (or moqui) is the old name for Hopi, and this Navajo blanket style is decidedly Hopi in origin. In fact, it is so originally Hopi that in many cases it is difficult to determine which people wove a particular piece.

The style is relatively plain. A serape-shaped wearing blanket, it has a dark, monontonous, narrow background of natural brown/black and indigo stripes interrupted by narrow bands of red or white. Beading, tiny vertical stripes of alternating dark and light colors, is sometimes present as well. The diamond shape was generally woven in the center (a remnant of the chief style) and, like the chief blanket, it gradually grew in complexity of design.

The banded style was woven at the same time as the Moki— in the 1870's. It is similar to the simple Moki style in that banded areas of color are interspersed at rhythmical intervals between solid areas of color. Again, the palette is limited to the naturals, indigo blue, the bayeta colors, and a few native yellows and greens.

Moki Blanket. *The Museum of the American Indian, New York. Heye Foundation.*

Banded Blanket. *The Museum of the American Indian, New York. Heye Foundation.*

THE LATE SERAPE STYLE

Although five years of incarceration put an end to the bayeta serape, the style continued in the 1870's without the essential bayeta colors. Called late serape, it included the elements of the early blankets, but began to include a terraced or T-shaped motif as well. The late serape style became so energetic and colorful through the use of new commercial materials, such as aniline dyes, that it soon exploded into the "eye dazzler."

Late Serape Style Blanket. *The Field Museum of Natural History, Chicago.*

THE END OF THE CLASSIC PERIOD

The opening of the West by the railroads in the 1880's marks the end of the classic period of Navajo weaving. It was "classic" in the sense that, although eclectic and changing, it still maintained a connection to native design, materials, and function, and it remained relatively free from the influence of the white culture. That sounds like an outright lie when one realizes that it was the Pueblo loom, Spanish sheep, and indigo dye, and English flannel that stimulated the growth of Navajo weaving, but the function and the quality of the blanket has not been equaled since that time.

THE BOOM OR TRANSITION PERIOD

What is known as a period of decadence set in during the late 1800's. Trading posts were established along railroad routes, and blankets fast became a popular trade item. Customers included many people who, not comprehending or needing the function of the blanket, asked for it to be made thicker for use as a floor covering.

Women became virtual slaves to the weaving market. Having been forced to settle in one place, dependent upon still meager flocks for meat and wool, women put full energy into making blankets and rugs for trade in an effort to pull their families out of impoverishment. Since the Navajos were provided with clothing by the government, weaving on the loom was directed primarily toward trade. The weaver was sometimes paid by the pound for her work—as little as twenty-five cents per pound! Considering that a blanket or rug takes many months of work and weighs about six pounds, you can understand why vegetable matter was frequently left in the yarn and why the blanket was sometimes weighted with sand after completion. This "pound rug," treated with so little respect by the trader and public, was carelessly and coarsely woven.

After the initial boom fostered by the railroad, business began to slack off due to the poor weaving quality. When the trader saw the reason, he took on the new role of savior of the blanket: he demanded higher standards and better design from the weavers, and he paid them a better price and encouraged the weaving of rugs.

EYE DAZZLERS

Eye Dazzler Blanket. *The Museum of the American Indian, New York. Heye Foundation.*

By the end of 1885 the railroads had brought many new materials to the reservation. Three items made important contributions to the stylistic development of the blanket: Germantown yarn, a domestic aniline-dyed, machine-spun yarn; Saxony yarn, an imported vegetable-dyed, machine-spun yarn; and packaged aniline dyes. Spurred by the freedom from a restricted color palette, and in many cases freed from the task of spinning her own yarn, the weaver found her interest in weaving rekindled.

The machine-spun yarn was much finer in comparison to the homespun, so while the scale of the weavings remained the same, the designs grew in complexity. The zigzag or lightning design became popular, and the radiating diamond expanded from its two-dimensional confines. The multiplication of simple shapes into labyrinths commanded the full attention of the weaver. She put so much of herself into the piece that between her energy, the colors, and the design the piece was literally eye-dazzling.

It is true that the quality of the work did not often equal that of the earlier blankets. But the spontaneity of color, the explosiveness of design, and the expressionism of the piece hardly merit the term "florid decadence," which I once heard applied to the style. Though it seems to have been too flamboyant for most tastes, the geometric style was nevertheless influential on 20th century American painters.

THE OUTLINE STYLE

The outline style developed concurrently with the eye dazzlers in the late 1880's. Indeed the style is very often considered part of the eye dazzler genre. The distinguishing characteristic is that the shapes are woven with fine lines of another color surrounding them.

The outline style indicates a real knowledge, intuitive or developed, of the way colors work in proportion and juxtaposition to one another. In fact, these pieces are among the most visually exciting and the colors sometimes appear to vibrate. Interestingly, the outline is a basic element of sandpainting, an art form developed long before weaving began.

Outline Style Blanket. *The Museum of the American Indian, New York. Heye Foundation.*

PICTORIAL WEAVING

Popular in the late 1880's, the pictorial blanket was the first to break from a history of abstract design. Rather than being placed within a pictorial context, however, the figure—cow, horse, bird, human, etc.—was treated as a design element and thus still maintained a tie to formal tradition. I think that is one reason why the figures remained angular, for certainly if the weavers had wanted to they could have rounded them out. G.W. James suggests that the lack of arches and circles is traced to the development of weaving from basketry, where because of the relative rigidity of the medium, corners are sharply pointed and lines are straight, angular, or serrated. (*Indian Blankets and their Makers,* p.121.)

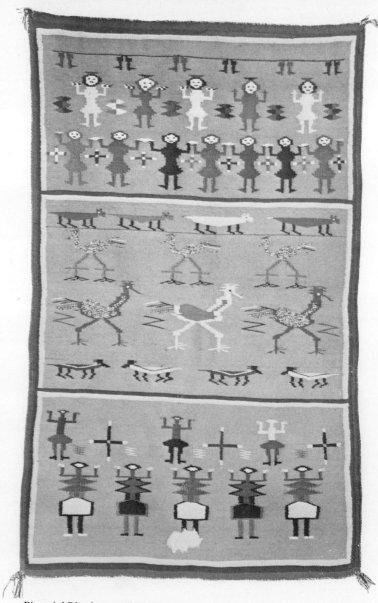

Pictorial Blanket, *c. 1890. The Museum of the American Indian, New York. Heye Foundation.*

THE YEI BLANKET

The Yei blanket was a direct outgrowth of pictorial weaving. Begun cautiously in the early 1900's, the style had to face strong tribal opposition because the Yei were Navajo divinities previously represented only on sacred sandpaintings. They were figures whose images were not meant to exist permanently, whose images on a secular object were regarded with extreme suspicion.

Slowly, this style of blanket came into its own. Though there are some sandpaintings reproduced on the loom, the majority of the figures are taken out of that context and placed in rather formal composition. Yet because the Yei blankets are seen in a pictorial sense rather than a purely abstract one, they have found their way to more walls than floors. The style continues today, where realistic human figures are often integrated with the angular divinities.

Yei-Bichai Blanket, *contemporary. The Museum of the American Indian, New York. Heye Foundation.*

THE RUG PERIOD

The rug period during the turn of the century got off to a more stable start than the previous period of design frenzy. Traders emphasized certain desirable qualities for rugs: natural hand-spun yarns, good weaving quality, and a complex but not ecstatic design. Though the styles and techniques are essentially in keeping with the Navajo tradition, a new element, the border, is introduced. It is this border that marks the final distinction between blanket and rug. It has been suggested that the border was adopted from the Oriental carpet as a means of distinguishing the woven rug from a blanket.

THE REVIVAL PERIOD

In the revival period, the decade between 1920 and 1930, the pure forms of the older styles were again considered for use. Natural dyeing was extensive, new colors were tried, and an attempt was made to use only the best. This fervor of improvement continues today, with contemporary Navajo weavers attempting (and succeeding) to bring their work up to the old standards of excellence.

CONTEMPORARY WEAVING

There is a current tendency for Navajo weavers to specialize in designs of their particular areas. Although it is not always the case (for some weavers prefer to create their own geometric patterns or realistic flower and animal motifs), contemporary weaving can generally be categorized according to the design types from specific areas.

In Two Grays Hills and Tees nos Pas, New Mexico, complex geometric designs with solid or figured borders are woven. In Two Gray Hills rugs the designs are extremely intricate. Colors are natural, with only the barest amount of pigment, and that is generally from vegetable-dyed yarns. The weft count is usually very high. Sometimes there are so many threads per inch that the finely woven pieces resemble blankets more than rugs in fineness and drapability.

Tees nos Pas rugs are not always as detailed. There is generally more color, sometimes vegetable-dyed but more often colored with aniline dyes. Yet even though many colors are often used, the effect is striking in its subtlety. The most common colors are in the red, orange, yellow, and green families.

In Ganado, Arizona, the weavers use a dark, rich red that has come to be associated so closely with the weaving there that it is called "Ganado red." It is the only dyed color used. The rest of the palette consists of white, browns, blacks, and the whole range of tans and grays in between. The style is most often bordered and very often complex, but the overall effect is one of boldness rather than complexity.

Pieces woven almost exclusively with vegetable-dyed, often hand-spun yarn are from several locations. Chinle, Arizona, weavers began the first revival of natural dyeing. The colors are muted, almost pastel-like vegetable shades. There, as well as at Wide Ruin, Arizona, rugs are woven in the banded style of the 1870's and adhere closely to the original designs and techniques. Crystal, New Mexico, rugs are also woven from

Individual Style Blanket, c. 1900. The Field Museum of Natural History, Chicago.

Terraced Diamond *by Inez Ettcity.*
Courtesy of American Indian Treas-
ures, Inc. Guilderland, New York.

Chief Blanket, *3rd phase, by Louise*
Preston, Black Mountain. Courtesy of
American Indian Treasures, Inc.

Ganado *(detail) weaver unknown. Courtesy of American Indian Treasures, Inc., New York.*

Banded Blanket *by Rena Touchine, Wide Ruin. Courtesy of American Indian Treasures, Inc., New York.*

Banded Blanket *(detail) by Louise Harrison. Courtesy of American Indian Treasures, Inc., New York.*

vegetable-dyed yarns with designs that are adaptions of the banded style. The pieces often contain fine wavy lines that distinguish them from the vegetable-dyed pieces of the other two areas.

Yei rugs are generally from the Shiprock and Lukachukai, Arizona, areas. Most often the Yeis are woven in a variety of colors with machine-spun aniline-dyed yarn. In Shiprock, sandpainting rugs are woven as well. Because of religious taboos (and I would imagine later because of the complexity of design) sandpaintings were not woven until around 1920. Even now a rug is not a true copy of a sandpainting. Certain details are either omitted or changed to comply with the cultural belief that a permanent sandpainting is bad luck. Although many rugs of this type are woven in commercial yarns for the tourist trade, there are some woven from specially carded blends of vegetable-dyed fleece that are classics in the genre.

Gallup, New Mexico, and Coal Mine Mesa, Arizona, are two centers for the production of twill blankets. Around Gallup these take the form of saddle blankets (generally no larger than 2x3 feet) with many variations of the twill weave—herringbone, bird's-eye, etc. At Coal Mine Mesa there is a double-faced weaving being done where the two sides of a piece show different designs.

This is by no means a complete description of contemporary weaving styles—far from it. Many productive and distinctive areas have been neglected but it was my hope that this will provide a general overview.

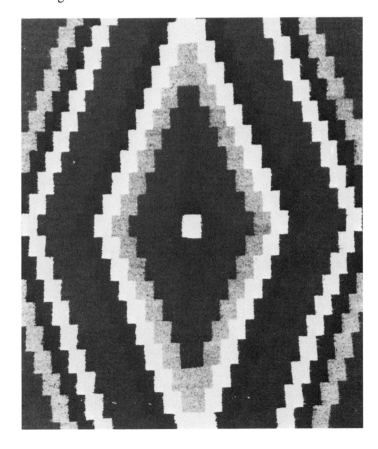

Ganado *(detail) weaver unknown. Courtesy of American Indian Treasures, Inc., New York.*

Three Women Working *on, from left to right, spinning, weaving, and carding. Photo by Ray Manley.*

WEAVING MATERIALS

No discussion of Navajo weaving materials could begin without a word about the sheep and the processes the fleece undergoes during its journey into yarn.

The sheep first used by the Navajos were merino, with abundant, silky wool, that were brought over by the Spanish colonists in the 16th and 17th centuries. Kit Carson and his raiders decimated this original flock in 1863. Subsequently the U.S. government provided the tribe with sheep to begin their flock anew. These were American sheep, imported originally from Britain; the fleece was curlier and denser than that of the merino.

Flocks of sheep differed somewhat, and still do, from area to area in the reservation, but there is a breed of mixed origin known as "Navajo sheep" that is the favorite of the weaver. Presumably it was bred from the government allotment of sheep, with the addition of various strains to improve the quality of the fleece. It is a small and hardy animal, with long, wavy fleece that produces a smooth yarn. The relatively greaseless state of the fleece makes it very desirable; when water was scarce there was no fleece to match it in cleanliness (the greasier a fleece, the greater the likelihood of its picking up dirt). Even today the tiresome chore of washing the fleece before carding is happily eliminated with this fleece.

SHEARING

The first step in the transition from fleece on the sheep to woven piece is shearing, when the fleece is separated from the animal. This is done in the early spring when the winter coat is still thick. Quite simply, the operation proceeds as follows: the shearer ties the legs of the animal together and proceeds to clip the fleece off the sheep from the back to the tail, down the sides, and then under the belly. The best wool comes from the sides because it is neither weathered, as on the back, nor matted and encrusted with vegetable and animal matter, as on the belly and tail. Originally shearing was done with crude knives, but today good hand or mechanical shears permit no wastage of wool.

Although it is rare, the fleece may be washed after shearing if it is unusually greasy. (This grease, lanolin in its unrefined state, is what prevents the fleece from matting together while on the animal. The grease content varies from breed to breed.)

Navajo Woman with Fleece, *1904. The Museum of the American Indian, New York. Heye Foundation.*

CARDING

Once separated from the animal, the mass of fleece is sorted for quality of fiber, picked for burrs and other vegetable matter, and then carded, or "combed," to straighten out the fibers and fluff them for spinning. Hand cards have always been used by Navajo weavers. One of the first forms of hand cards were teasles (thistles) set into a wooden frame. Later, the Navajos used cards similar to those in use today. They have metal teeth set into a leather foundation which is in turn set onto a wood backing with a handle attached.

The carder holds one card in each hand, with the teeth of each card facing the other. She lays a bit of fleece on the bottom card and then moves the top card across it without the teeth touching. The process requires great strength since the fleece sandwiched between the cards is literally being pulled in opposite directions. Carding not only efficiently straightens out the fibers, but helps to further clean the wool by loosening additional bits of dirt and matter.

Teasels. *Early cards were made from teasels set into a wood frame.*

SPINNING

Once the wool is carded the spinner can begin. Although shearing and carding processes have improved through technology, the spindle remains unchanged. As in the nomadic days, it is a dowel-like stick about 2 feet long with a wooden (or sometimes sandstone) whorl attached about 6″ from the bottom.

Very simply, the spinning operation proceeds in the following manner. The spinner sits or kneels on the ground, her spindle at her right side. The point of the spindle pivots on the ground while the top rests against her thigh. Feeding carded fleece with her left hand, she pushes the spindle along her thigh with her right hand. As the spindle turns it catches the carded wool and spins it into a loose yarn. The yarn is wound around the shaft of the spindle as it is spun. The spinner makes enough yarn for her whole project.

Three types of yarn are needed for the traditional Navajo piece. For the warp yarn, the spinner respins her yarn twice after the initial spinning to obtain a thin, tightly spun yarn that will withstand tension and constant beating. The weft yarn, spun only once after the initial spinning, is softer and more pliant. This yarn determines the textural quality of the woven piece. The third type of yarn is used only at the selvedges for the bound edge must be quite strong. This yarn is spun twice and then plied (two threads are spun together, each twisting around the other).

Tools. *This photo shows fleece cards, and spindles.*

Color

Most weaving was initially done with natural white, natural brown/black, and the grays resulting from mixing the two. Any wool that was dyed was done so after spinning. Contrary to common belief, native dyes were used very sparingly until the beginning of the 20th century, when experimentation in that area was intense.

There were some dyes, however, made from simple scrub brushes and weeds, that were used early in weaving. Mordants, the chemicals needed to "fix" the colors, were natural alum, obtained from crystals found in recently washed-out areas, and juniper ashes.

Black. Sumac leaves, rich in tannic acid, provided a good black dye. Used mainly for tanning hides, sumac was also used to darken the natural brown/black yarn to a more consistent hue. It was especially popular because the tannic acid required no mordant.

Yellow. Several native dyeplants were counted on to give good consistent results: wild carrot, rabbitbrush, and sagebrush. They produced a range of colors from orange-yellow to yellow-green, and they were included in some of the earliest weaving.

Green. This color was obtained by using the native yellow dyes together with indigo.

Blue. There is evidence that indigo was in use almost at the beginning of the Navajo weaving era because it is found in some of the earliest blankets. Indigo coloring matter was rendered from the leaves of a plant in the pea family. Shipped by the Spanish to the Southwest, it reached the Pueblos at an early date, and the Navajos shortly thereafter.

Red. Red was a difficult color to produce with native dyestuffs. Mahogany bark, alder, and sumac root gave a pale red to a reddish-brown, but with the availability of bayeta cloth, the existing natural dyes were scarcely used.

Aniline Dyes. The synthetic aniline dyes reached the weaver via the railroad in the beginning of the 1880's. They were inexpensive and easy to use: color and mordant came in one packet that was dropped whole into boiling water to unleash any one of a number of beautiful and not-so-beautiful colors. After that the weaver merely dropped her hand-spun yarn into the dye-bath.

Bayeta

Bayeta was a woolen flannel cloth woven in England and brought to the Southwest by the Spanish as a peace offering and trade item. Although it came in other colors, it was the red that caught the fancy of the Navajo weaver, due in part to the fact that there was no true red available from the dyestuffs. (On rare occasions bayeta yellow or green was also used.)

Bayeta was dyed a fine carmine or ruby red with cochineal, a dye made from the pulverized shells of an insect that lives on the opuntia cactus. Because the insect is not common to the United States and because the color was so fine, weavers took

to unraveling the fabric and reweaving the strands into their own work. Sometimes they used the strands singly, but they more often re-plied the filaments into a thicker fiber. In the very early days of bayeta, the cloth was sometimes cut into strips and woven.

The fine, even twist of this thin, strong thread was an inspiration for the weavers' own spinning. It is no wonder that the bayeta blanket is considered a classic; its materials are no longer in existence.

YARNS

Bayeta gradually disappeared during the Navajos' imprisonment at Bosque Redondo, but it was never forgotten, so when the first skeins of a vegetable-dyed, machine-spun, three-ply yarn with a tight, fine twist came west with the white traders, the weavers took to it readily.

Saxony. Imported from Germany, this yarn was as expensive as it was fine. It was consequently used sparingly, and it was not until the appearance of a domestic yarn ten years later, in the 1880's, that this type of yarn came into popular use.

Germantown. Named after its place of manufacture in Germantown, Pennsylvania, this yarn was an aniline-dyed, machine-spun yarn available in either three- or four-ply weights. Still much more expensive than homespun, it nevertheless was used as the prime material in many of the eye dazzlers, that style that was the bane of tasteful consumers. Needless to say, it was available in a very wide range of colors.

Cotton. Cotton twine warp yarn came into use briefly because it was tight, relatively strong, and already spun, as well as inexpensive. It was the base of many a Germantown eye dazzler. When traders and customers alike realized that its wearing properties did not begin to approach the durability of wool, however, it was quickly retracted from the shelves.

WHAT IS USED TODAY

Largely because of the efforts of the weavers during the revival period, and through the continuing work of contemporary weavers, hand-spun yarn in natural colors has made a comeback as the primary ingredient of the Navajo rug. There is also a sizeable amount of natural-dyed color in the woven piece. While aniline dyes sometimes appear in hand-spun yarn, and more than occasionally a commercially spun yarn appears, both are used with restraint and great skill. A common color combination is natural white, grays, and aniline-dyed red. The natural brown/black is commonly darkened to a uniform black with anilines.

Saddle Blanket *in the comb pattern made of Germantown wool yarns. The Museum of the American Indian, New York, Heye Foundation.*

Navajo Women Working. *Here one woman works at the loom while the other spins. Photo by Ray Manley.*

MAKING THE LOOM

The Navajo loom is basically an upright taptestry loom. Throughout history many of the major textiles of the world have been woven on looms of this family—from the brocaded cloths of Nigeria to the intricate pile rugs of the East and the tapestries of medieval Europe.

The loom has not changed appreciably since prehistoric times. It is so functionally perfect that it can scarcely be improved upon; any structural changes are minor and do not interfere with the basic principle.

In Navajo weaving, a new loom is made at the outset of each project that corresponds to the specifications of the new piece. The loomframe has traditionally been made by lashing together piñon branches or saplings. The loom was easily disassembled, a necessity in the nomadic days. Today the loom is often set up permanently indoors. In a simple variation of the frame, the top of each upright culminates in a Y-shape from the fork of a tree, which allows the top crosspiece to rest in the crotch. Sometimes the uprights are two trees growing at a convenient distance apart, and outdoor looms are still set up in this manner today.

The adaptability of the loom is borne out by the fact that it functions equally well with many substitutions in material—cut lumber for the frame; broomsticks, shovel handles, dowels, or metal pipes for the crosspieces and beams; and twine or baling wire for the bindings.

If you are interested in setting up a loom of this type, you have two alternatives. You can construct a traditional loom of the type the Navajos use, or you might build yourself a contemporary variation using materials from the lumberyard, the barn, or your workshop. The following description is for the traditional loom, but Chapter 6 presents a number of variations of the loom and methods for making it stand upright. Chapters 7 and 8 present variations in warping, heddle making, and alternative techniques and materials.

The Sampler. If you are unfamiliar with Navajo looms or weaving techniques, I suggest that you set up your first loom to correspond to the sampler of weaves presented in Chapter 5. The sampler is 10" wide by 26" long, so the top of rod **F** of your loom should be positioned 26" away from the bottom of rod **E**. The warp is unbleached cotton string set at 6 ends per inch. The Frame of the loom should be at least one foot longer and wider than the planned weaving.

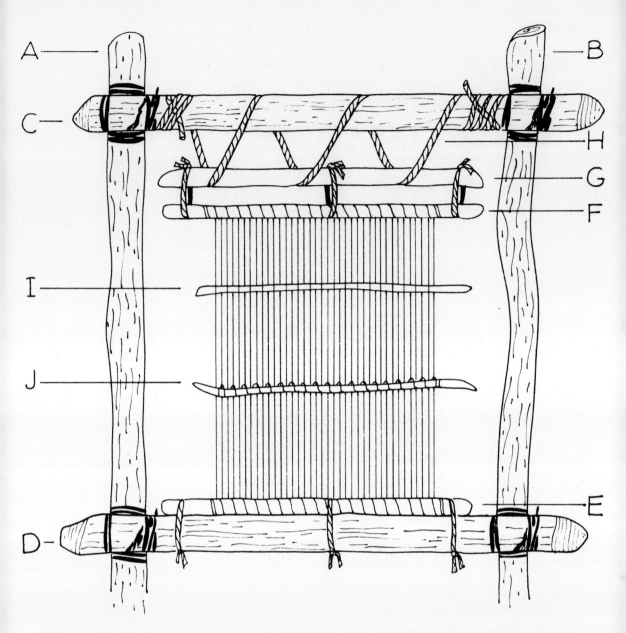

Figure 1. *Here are the parts of a traditional loom: the upright posts (A and B), the crosspieces (C and D), sticks or dowels for the moveable frame (E, F, and G), the shed stick (I), the heddle rod (J), heavy rope for tying on (H), and thin twine for binding, and finally, the warp yarn.*

MATERIALS

The following list will give you general guidelines for all the components that go into putting together a traditional loom:

The Upright Posts. These should be of fairly heavy wood and equal in length. The bark can be removed if desired, but this is not necessary.

The Crosspieces. These must be very smooth, heavy pieces of wood of equal length.

The Movable Loom. For this you need three strong, straight sticks that are longer than the width of the warp and at least 1″ in diameter.

The Heddle rod. This should be a stout rod or dowel at least ¾″ in diameter.

The Shed Rods. Two dowels or reeds ½″ in diameter are needed.

Rope and Twine. You will need heavy rope or clothesline to secure the dowels to the crosspieces. Leather thongs can also be used for lashing the uprights and crosspieces. Thin, strong twine is needed for binding the warp to the dowels, for the heddles, and for tying the loom into the frame.

Warp. The Navajo weaver uses a tightly spun one-ply wool. A good alternate material is strong cotton string.

THE FRAME

The loom is composed of two parts—the loom frame and the moveable loom (see Figure 1). For the loom frame, two upright posts (A and B) are spanned horizontally by two crosspieces (C and D) near the top and bottom. The frame should be made with corners as near to 90° as possible, and the wood should be secured by lashing the pieces together with rawhide strips or ropes. Some weavers cut out two sections of each upright to allow the crosspieces to fit securely (Figure 2). The whole frame should be roughly one foot larger by each dimension than the piece to be woven.

Lashing. Lashing with a strong cord is a relatively simple method of joining things in a strong but temporary way. Rawhide thongs are excellent to use, particularly if you wet them before using since they will later shrink and make a very tight join.

THE MOVEABLE LOOM

The moveable loom is the area within the loom frame that holds the warp (stretched between dowels E and F) and the means for lowering it or adjusting the tension (rod G). The moveable loom is assembled after the warp has been wound around a temporary frame.

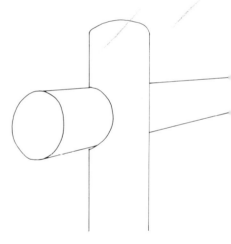

Figure 2. *You can bind the frame by cutting out two sections of each upright and inserting the crosspieces.*

Lashing 1. *(Above) Wind the rope twice around the upright. Insert the free end under the wind and pull tight.*

2. *(Left) Wrap the tail around the free end of rope to prevent its working loose.*

3. *(Above) Then wrap the free end under and behind the upright, over to the left side of the crosspiece, and around the other upright, over to the left side of the crosspiece, and around the other upright. Pull tight after each movement, and repeat three times.*

4. *(Left) Now wrap circularly around the crosspieces and over the uprights as shown. Pull tight after each movement and repeat the process three times.*

5. *To finish, make two wraps around a crosspiece and slip through the loose end. Pull tight and lashing is complete.*

6. *Here is your finished frame.*

The Warping Frame

The warp threads are stretched on a warping frame before being transferred to two dowels and secured to the loom. The warping frame consists of a second set of both uprights and crosspieces. These can be scrap wood, but the crosspieces *must* be smooth. The size of the frame is determined by the dimensions of the warp, but it is generally large enough to enclose both the warp and the weaver.

The uprights, named for simplicity's sake, are actually set horizontally on blocks, flat stones, or bricks to raise the frame about 3″ or so from the ground. Then dowels or smooth sticks are set parallel to each other as crosspieces. The distance from the top of the top dowel to the bottom of the bottom dowel is the length of the warp. Check carefully to make sure that the distance between the crosspieces is the same at both sides or the warp will be uneven. (The loom frame may occasionally be a little less than square, but the warp frame must *never* be). The uprights and crosspieces are then lashed together.

Once the warping frame is assembled, four large nails—one in each corner—are driven about a third of the way into the uprights to prevent the crosspieces from moving forward during warping. When warping is completed the frame can be disassembled for later use with another warp.

The warping frame.

The Warp

The threads that form the warp are the foundation of the woven piece. They are the most important element of the pre-weaving process, for without them there could be no woven piece. In Navajo weaving, the warp is strung from a continuous length of yarn. Individual threads are spaced anywhere from 5 to 20 ends per inch, with 8 being a common and comfortable number to work with.

Figuring out the correct amount of warp needed is easy, although the Navajo woman can calculate the amount she needs by weight and feel. The number of warp ends per inch is multiplied by the number of inches wide the piece will be (for example, 8 ends per inch by 10″ wide). That number (80) is then multiplied by the number of inches in the length of the warp (say 30″, which equals 2,400″). That final number divided by 12 will yield the length of warp in feet; divided by 36 will yield the length in yards.

Warping. The Navajo weaver sits inside the warping frame. The first step is to bring the warp thread, wound in a ball or around a stick, around the top dowel and tie it to itself with a simple knot. Proceeding to the bottom dowel, she takes the thread over it, then under it, then up to the top dowel, and the process is repeated. From the side the whole thing looks like a series of continuous figure-eights (Figure 3).

The weaver is conscious of two things: spacing and tension. Spacing for 8 epi (ends per inch), for example, the weaver places her threads ¼″ apart as she goes around the dowel, since that turn represents two warp threads. When the desired width is reached, the weaver ends at the bottom dowel by tying the end of yarn to the last warp string.

An even tension must be maintained throughout the warping for an even weaving surface. A good weaver can run her hand lightly over the warp and feel any discrepancies. A beginner must be more discerning, but can do the same thing. If the weaver does find that one or more ends are tighter or looser than the others after she has tied the warp off, the solution is simple. Starting at the tightest part, the weaver works toward the loose end by gently tugging each string to the tension of the previous one. But the time she has reached the other end, the extra warp thread is broken off and the warp is retied.

Inserting the Shed Rods. Two reeds, sticks, or dowels about ½″ in diameter are used for the shed rods. One rod is inserted in the space formed by the warp threads at the top, the second in the space formed at the bottom. Each is pushed toward the middle where the warp strands cross. The sticks are then tied together at each end. They will preserve the order of crossed threads for later steps.

Figure 3. *The warp is wound in a figure-eight pattern.*

The weaver winds the warp around the frame in a figure-eight pattern.

Put one shed rod through each space formed by the crossed threads, then bring the rods toward the center of the warp.

TWINING

Twining is an ancient basketry technique wherein a doubled weft encircles each warp. It is used here for its technical qualities as a warp spacer and selvedge strengthener. The cord for twining should be chosen carefully because it must either contrast or blend with the colors of the weft; many times it is the color of the warp. It is also chosen for its diameter: a thicker yarn will leave larger spaces between warp ends, while a thinner yarn will allow more threads per inch. (A thinner yarn can also be twisted more than once between warp threads to create more space.) The twining cord is cut about three times the width of the warp and doubled. An overhand knot is tied about 3″ in from the loop, and twining can begin.

Twining is started just above the bottom dowel. Using only the warp threads on top of the dowel, the weaver encircles the first warp thread with her two twining cords. She twists the cords, then encircles the second thread (Figure 4). The twining is pushed to the bottom of the dowel as it moves along, and the process is repeated until the last warp thread is reached. The twining cords are then tied off with an overhand knot, and the twining is repeated at the top dowel.

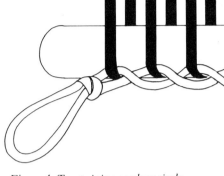

Figure 4. *Two twining cords encircle each warp with a twist in-between.*

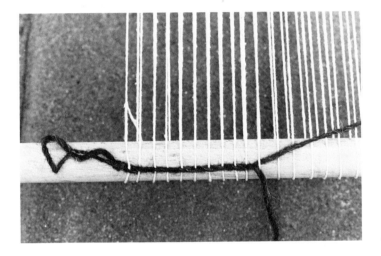

Here is the twining in progress.

When twining is complete, the warp will be evenly spaced along the dowel.

BINDING THE WARP ONTO NEW DOWELS

Since the Navajo blanket has selvedges (self-edges) bound by twining on all four sides, this step is one of pure genius. A very smooth stick or dowel is lined up adjacent to the bottom dowel of the warping frame. Taking a darning needle, sacking needle, or a makeshift substitution, and threading it with a strong, thin cord (cotton twine, for example), the weaver ties the cord to the end of the new dowel and begins to sew the warp to it. The thread goes in between the warp threads and around the new dowel, and in effect binds the twining to the second dowel. When the weaver is finished with one end, she takes another dowel and repeats the process at the other end.

When the weaver has completed the process at both ends the warp is firmly bound between the new dowels. The old warp frame dowels are removed from the warp. The new warp frame dowels and the warp are now independent of the warping frame, and the warp is ready to be set into the loom frame.

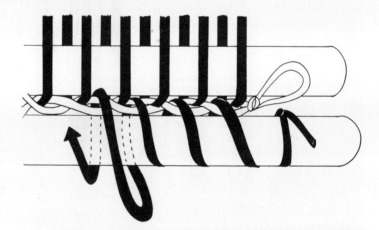

Figure 5. *The new dowel is attached to the twining in this manner.*

The twining has been pushed to the bottom of the dowel and the new dowel is attached to it.

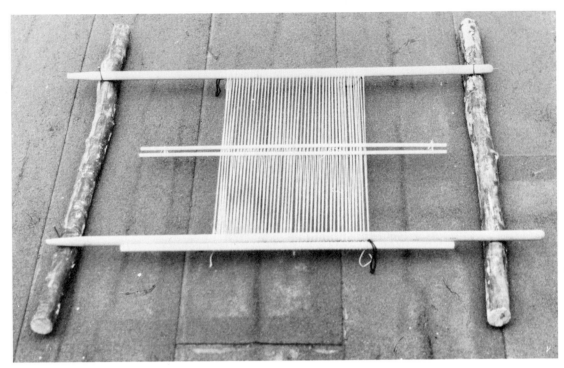

Here is an overview of the warping frame and one new dowel.

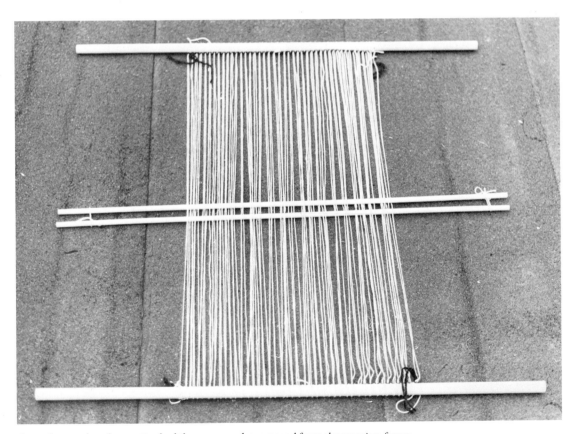

Once the new dowels are attached the warp can be removed from the warping frame.

SETTING THE WARP INTO THE FRAME

The loom frame should be standing upright. The weaver takes the finished warp and attaches the dowel from one end of it to crosspiece D of the loom frame. The warp dowel is tied to the frame with string, twine, or baling wire in the middle and at both ends. At this point the dowel is labeled E and is known as the cloth beam.

The dowel at the other end of the warp consequently becomes rod F or the warp beam. The weaver now attaches the warp beam to rod G. All three ties should be made evenly, at a distance of about 3″

The final step in making the loom proper is to bind rod G to the top crosspiece C by a method that regulates the warp tension and allows the warp to be lowered as the weaving progresses. The weaver uses a long length of rope or clothesline. She starts at the extreme left of crosspiece C and wraps the rope twice around it, tucking the tail end under the loops (see Figure 6). She then begins to lace C and G together, going behind the back of both and down to the bottom of G, up the front of both beams, and over the top of crosspiece C, etc. She finishes by making two loops, inserting the loose end underneath, and pulling tight. As tension is exerted on these moorings they pull tighter. The excess rope will be needed later to lower the warp.

Tension should be taut and even throughout. If it is not, the weaver goes back to the rope and begins to pull here, tug there, to even out the warp. Then she resecures.

Just as the loom has been easily assembled, it can be easily dismantled. No doubt this is why it was so readily accepted by the then-nomadic Navajos.

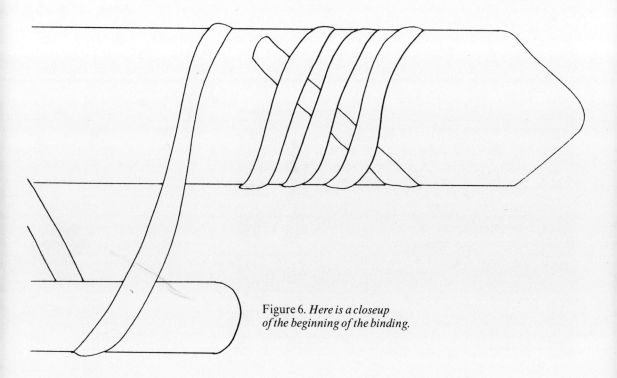

Figure 6. *Here is a closeup of the beginning of the binding.*

The cloth beam is attached to the bottom crosspiece with heavy twine.

The warp beam is attached to another crosspiece (Rod G).

Rod G is attached to the top crosspiece of the loom with heavy twine.

Making the Sheds

All that is left to do on the loom is to establish a way whereby the two sheds, held by shed rods 1 and 2, can be alternately opened. Making the first shed is simple. A flat stick, longer that the width of the warp and about 1½″ wide, is inserted into the space occupied by the top shed rod. Turned on its end, this stick makes a shed the width of its 1½″.

The process for making the second shed is a bit more involved. The threads held by shed rod 2 come from the back of the warp and are held rigidly in front. With two sheds in front this way, no weaving can occur because there can be no shed alternation. So, the following process describes how the threads from the back can be pulled forward to form the second shed and then relaxed.

The weaver needs a ½″ to ¾″ dowel or stick and a small ball of string. The end of this string is carried from right to left completely through the shed made by shed rod 2. The string is then attached loosely to the right end of the dowel, from now on called the heddle rod. The weaver begins with the warp threads of the second shed brought forward by shed rod 2. Starting at the left of the warp, the weaver begins to make heddles or loops with the string by catching it with the index finger of her right hand between the first two warp threads in front of the shed rod. She then pulls it into a loop and twists it and slips it on to the heddle rod (Figure 7). The space between the heddle rod and the warp threads (the length of the loops) should be about 1″. As more heddles are made they are all pushed further left on the dowel. The weaver continues to the end of the warp and then ties off. The process is finished by pulling out shed rod 2 but leaving shed rod 1 in place. It is important to restate that the heddle-making process takes place only with the set of warps in front of shed rod 2.

The weaver makes her second shed opening by pulling the heddle rod toward her and inserting the batten that was used to make the first shed. The batten is then withdrawn and the first shed can be made again. More about making the sheds will be found in the next chapter.

Figure 7. *Heddles are made by looping string through the warp strands and around the dowel or heddle rod.*

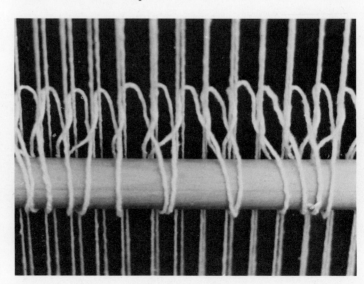

Here is a closeup of the heddles and the heddle rod.

The completed loom now only needs heddles and a shed stick.

Pillow *by Judy Junge. Soumack, a Middle-Eastern rug technique, is used here along with the traditional Navajo elements of beading and combing.*

USING THE LOOM

Before we discuss weaving, some information on tools is necessary. Every Navajo weaver has a set of many tools; this set, or parts of it, are often handed down from mother to daughter.

Batten. The batten, or sword, is given much attention since it is the tool that defines the sheds. Made from hardwood, it is generally about 27" long and 1½" wide. The thickness is about ⅜" at the top edge, tapering to somewhat less at the bottom. It is curved slightly at one end to facilitate inserting it between warp threads. Many weavers have a set of battens of differing widths, for instance, 1½", 1", and ½". (Substitutions for the batten are discussed in Chapter 6.)

Weaving Fork. Also made of hardwood, the weaving fork comes in several sizes and shapes. Since its function is to beat the weft down once it is laid in the shed, the fork must be fairly heavy. (Substitutions for the weaving fork are discussed in Chapter 6.)

Shuttle. The Navajo method of laying the yarn in the shed is done primarily with the hands, using short lengths of the spun fiber. Sometimes the yarn is wound into little balls. Since a good deal of Navajo weaving is done between the selvedges it is not surprising that a proper shuttle is not used. A stick of greasewood with yarn wrapped around it is occasionally passed through the shed in selvedge-to-selvedge weaving. Actually a stick of any material will suffice. (Shuttle variations are discussed in Chapter 7.)

Darning or Sacking Needle or Umbrella Rib. Aside from binding the warp to the cloth and warp beams, these tools are used as shuttles to carry the yarn at the end of the weaving process when the sheds can hardly be opened.

WEAVING

First, the weaver must be comfortable at her loom. She generally sits or kneels on a pillow or a pile of sheepskins or blankets on the floor or ground in front of the loom.

Just before actually weaving, the Navajo weaver does two things. First she cuts a length of edging cord somewhat more than twice the length of the warp. She doubles it around the crosspiece and cloth beams, rods D and E, and ties it loosely to the warp beam, rod F. This extra cord will make the whipped edge that runs the length of the blanket on both sides. It is discussed fully in Chapter 5.

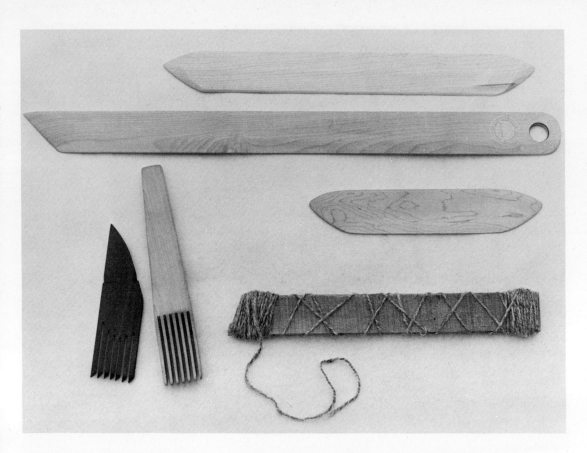

Here are various types of battens and weaving forks. At the bottom right is a stick shuttle.

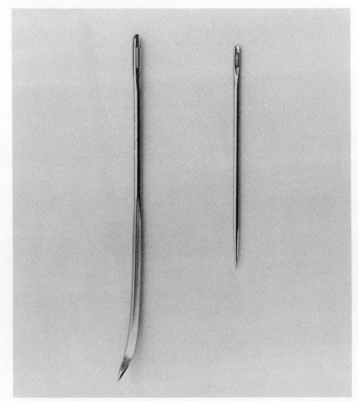

Sacking and darning needles.

Next the weaver breaks up the pairs of warp threads (formed by the twining) by putting the weft in with her fingers. Weaving two warps at a time, under one, over two and three, under four and five, she works to the end of the row (Figure 8). Coming back in the other direction she works just the opposite, going under where the first row went over. After the threads are separated with four rows of pairs weaving at the top and bottom the weaving can begin.

The Stick Shed. The weaver inserts her batten into the top (and only visible) shed or opening, from now on referred to as the stick shed. She does so just under the row of heddles. She turns the batten on edge and inserts the yarn at a slight diagonal angle. (Some weavers prefer to scallop the yarn.) She beats down the weft with her fork and removes the batten. Either method prevents the yarn from being pulled too tight in the shed.

The Pull Shed. For the second shed, from now on referred to as the pull shed, the weaver pulls the heddles toward her until the opening is large enough to insert the batten. Turning the batten on end, the weft is again laid diagonally in the shed. She beats the weft, withdraws the batten, and makes the first shed, the stick shed, again.

This process of opening the sheds and laying in the weft yarn is done in a continuous rhythmical motion rather than as a series of short movements. Part of this rhythm comes from practice—knowing the feel of the warp threads and the proper tension of the warp and weft. Another part is learning to maneuver the tools—holding the fork comfortably and not putting it down between shots, picking up the correct threads with the batten, and handling the batten. Speed and accuracy come with experience and time.

The stick shed is made by inserting the batten in the top (visible) shed and turning the batten on edge.

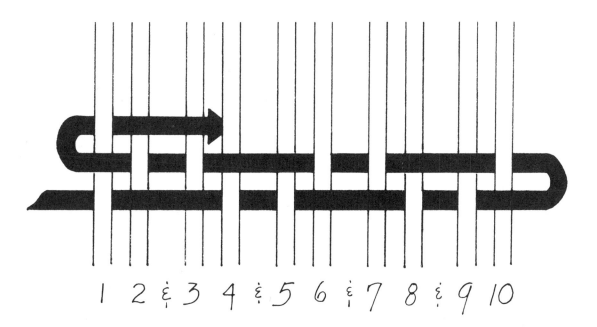

Figure 8. *Before weaving, the warp threads must be separated into pairs by the weft thread.*

The pull shed is made by pulling out the heddle rod and inserting the batten in the created opening.

Here is the open pull shed with the batten turned on edge.

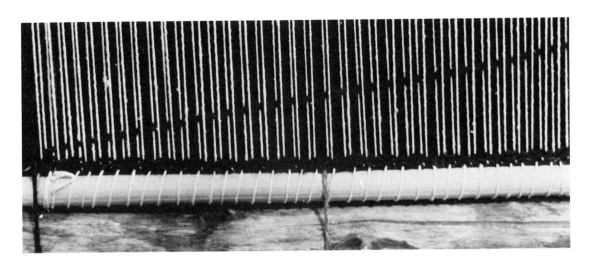

(Top) The weft thread is inserted at an angle to prevent the warp from being pulled in too tightly.

(Above) The weft then gets beaten down all across the warp width with the weaving fork.

For the first few rows, one strand of the edging cord is caught by the weft while the other is ignored.

WEAVING PARTICULARS

Sometimes the batten is not long enough to extend the full width of the weaving. If that is the case, the weaver inserts her batten in the first part of the shed and lays in the weft. She then moves the batten over to the next section of warp and opens that part of the shed. She continues in this manner until the weft is laid in the entire width of the weaving.

Problems with warping, broken threads, tension, and uneven weaving are discussed in Chapter 9.

Adding New Threads. If the weaver runs out of weft yarn in the middle of a row, a new length is added by overlapping it with the old weft for about four warp threads (Figure 9).

A new color is added by breaking the old weft at the end of a row, leaving a tail of yarn. The shed is changed, the tail of the old color tucked in and a new color inserted. On the next shed the tail of the new color is woven in (Figure 10).

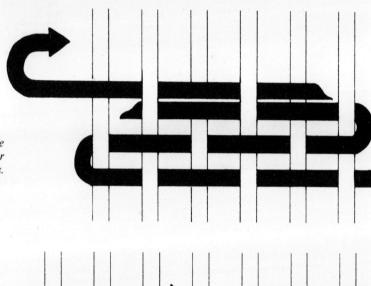

Figure 9. *To join threads in the middle of a row, the ends should overlap for several warps.*

Figure 10. *To begin a new color, the beginning and ending yarn tails must be tucked into opposite sheds.*

As the Weaving Progresses. As the weaving increases in height the weaver's arms get tired from reaching up. She has four ways to deal with the problem. If it is a small weaving she can sit successively higher, adding another pillow, then using a stool.

In the next three solutions the same first step is taken: using adjustment rope H, the weaver lowers her weaving by the same amount as she has woven. She then resecures the rope, unties the cloth beam, rolls the completed weaving around itself, and finally resecures the cloth beam to the bottom cross piece. Another solution is to sew the rolled part to itself before resecuring to the crosspiece. The third method is to untie the cloth beam, as in the two previous methods and bring it and the woven piece around the bottom crosspiece. The weaver can then either lash it to the upright posts in back or set the cloth beam on pegs or nails put in specially to hold it at that height (Figure 11).

For all three methods the weaver must adjust the tension of rope H before beginning to weave again. The weaver adjusts the height of the weaving as often as she needs to be comfortable at the loom. Do not be confused by old photographs of weavers at the loom where the woven section extends well beyond the weaver's reach. The blanket was unrolled for display.

Working with a Smaller Shed. As more and more of the warp area is covered by the weft, the shed space gets smaller. When it is too difficult to use a regular batten the weaver switches to successively smaller battens (1", then ½"), and next to small-diameter reeds or dowels. Finally, in roughly the last four inches, she is forced to manipulate the warp strings without the heddles or shed stick. She puts her weft in with a darning needle or umbrella rib and her fingers. She pushes rather than beats the weft down with a fine-tined fork.

One of the marks of a good weaver is how well she puts in the weft in the top few rows of weaving. There should be no noticeable mark. If you are contemplating this problem in your own weaving, I suggest that just when you think you could not possibly put in another row of weft, press it harder and add another three rows.

Finally the weaving is done. The cord binding the warp to dowels E and F is either cut or pulled out, and the weaving emerges as a self-contained woven piece.

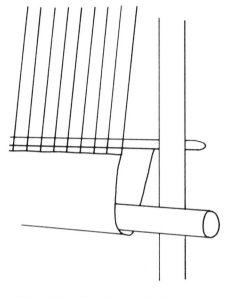

Figure 11. *Adjust the weaving by moving the cloth beam and woven piece around to the back of the loom.*

This is the sampler you will weave according to the instructions in this chapter.

WEAVING TECHNIQUES

The main characteristic of Navajo weaving is its stiff, heavy feel and appearance. This heaviness occurs because the warp is completely covered by the weft, each shot being securely pressed down to meet the previous row. With few exceptions, the technique used in Navajo weaving is weft-face plain weave. As you saw in the previous chapter, plain weave is the very simple procedure of laying the yarn in the two alternating sheds. Tapestry is a form of plain weave since the same shed alternation occurs. The difference is that in tapestry, the weft thread does not necessarily extend to the full weaving width; rather, it covers back and forth within a limited design or color area. This building up of weft color gradually forms the design.

This chapter will present a sampler of the various plain weaves and tapestry techniques. If you are unfamiliar with these techniques, I suggest you try your hand at the sampler using any loom with which you are familiar. If you are setting up a Navajo loom for the first time, this is a good opportunity to prepare the warp and heddles according to the instructions in Chapter Three. If you are in doubt as to what size to make your loom, remember to make the frame at least one foot longer and wider than the proposed weaving.

My sampler is 10″ wide by 26″ long, a comfortable size to begin with, and I suggest you follow a similar format.

For the warp I used unbleached cotton string set at 6 ends per inch. For the weft, I used a two-ply weaving yarn in black, white, and gray so the sampler would reproduce clearly. You could also use a thick one-ply yarn in natural or complementary colors (red/green, orange/blue, violet/yellow). A neutral color (gray, beige, or white) will work as the third color for the spaces in between. Weaving or tapestry yarn is best for the project, but four-ply knitting worsted will do in a pinch. If the yarn is too fine you will spend many hours filling your warp; too thick and you will not be able to see the subtleties of some of the techniques. I have not suggested using a one-ply, tightly spun yarn for the warp as is used traditionally in Navajo weaving because, for a first project, you will find the yarn difficult to handle.

The Sampler. After you have prepared your loom, assemble your tools and yarns. When you are ready, weave 2″ of plain weave (A) in a solid color. Beat the weft firmly with your fork or comb.

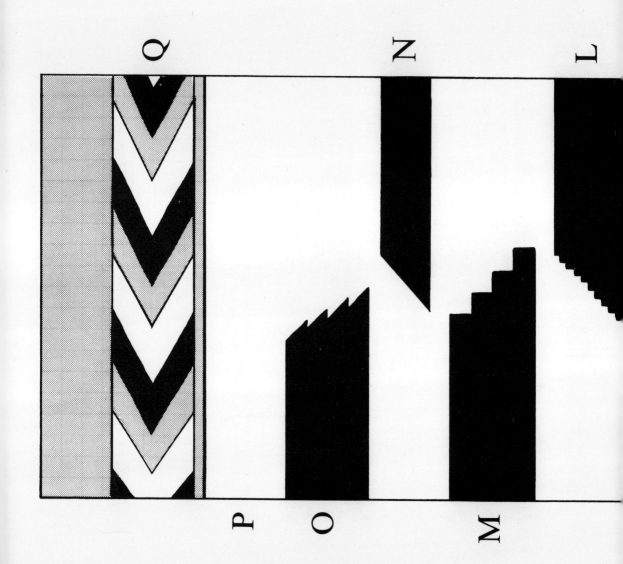

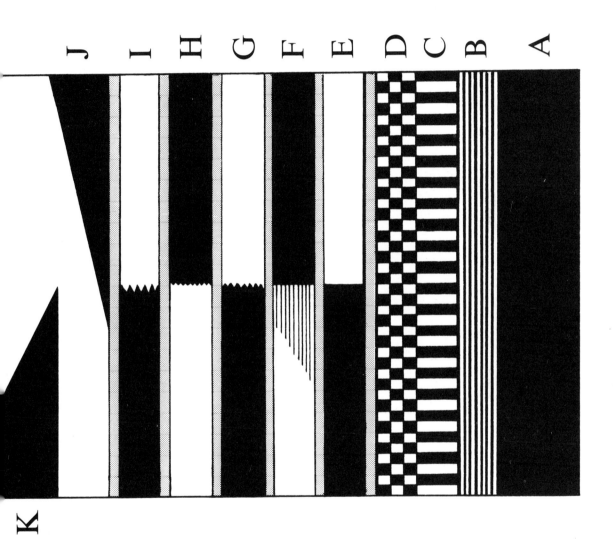

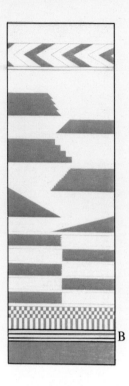

B

Fine Horizontal Stripes (B)

This is the simplest variation of plain weave. Use two shuttles, each of a different color. Start with color A and go through the stick shed, then back through the pull shed. Now take color B, and starting from the opposite end of the warp, take it through the stick shed and pull shed. This rhythmical alternation of colors produces fine stripes. Bear in mind that the finer the yarn, the finer the stripes will be. Notice that the stripes are slightly wavy, hence the technique is also known as wavy lines.

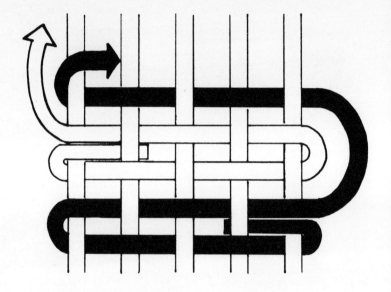

The Sampler. Introduce a second color and weave 1″ of fine horizontal stripes.

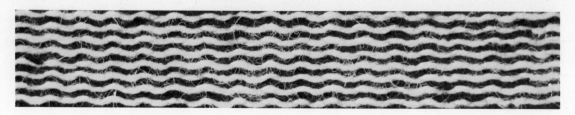

BEADING (C)

Use two shuttles, each wound with a different color. Color A always goes through the stick shed. Color B alternates, always going through the pull shed. Look carefully at the illustrations to see how the weft thread turns around the warp at the selvedge. Color B crosses over color A to "lock" color B at the selvedge (1). Color A then goes through the stick shed. Color B now goes through the opposite shed (2). At the selvedge, color B crosses over color A, and now both selvedges are "locked" (3). This crossing should be followed after every shot of weft. Try not to pull the weft too tight or the selvedges will pull in.

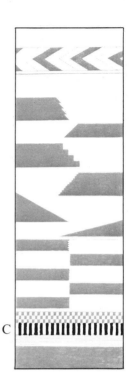

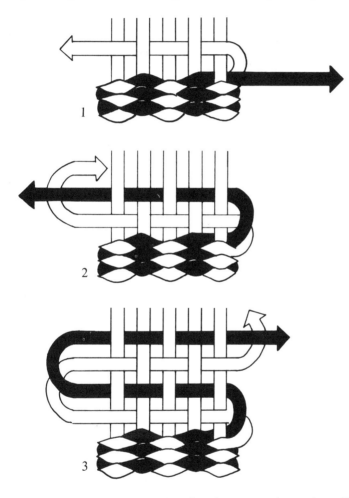

The Sampler. Weave 1″ of beading in contrasting colors. If beading is continued for more than ½″, the technique is often called warpway stripes.

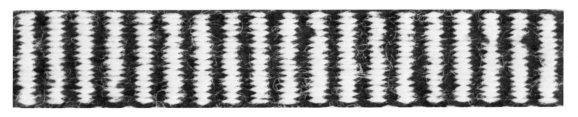

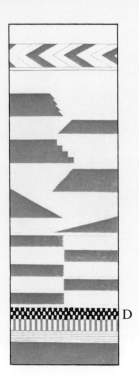

ALTERNATING BLOCKS (D)

Blocks are simply a variation of beading. First throw a shot of color A in its proper shed. Next, throw color A again in the pull shed, which puts color A where color B was and vice versa. The colors are now in the proper sheds to make blocks, and regular shed alternation continues until you want to change the color sequence back to its original order. The selvedges should be treated in the same way as for beading.

D

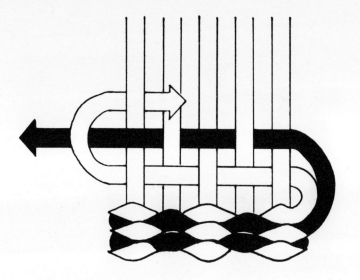

The Sampler. Weave three sets of alternating blocks. Then Weave ½″ of plain weave to prepare for the next section.

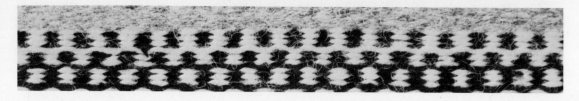

SLIT TAPESTRY (E)

The simplest tapestry method of weaving with two colors is the slit. Color A goes to a predetermined warp end, encircles it, then stops while color B is brought from the opposite end of the warp to the warp end adjoining color A. The shed is changed, and both colors turn around and go back to the selvedges. The shed is again changed and the process repeated. This method produces a slit in the weaving between the two colors that can be decoratively appealing, but is often functionally inadequate. When a neck slit it to be woven in a poncho, however, it is the only possible technique to use.

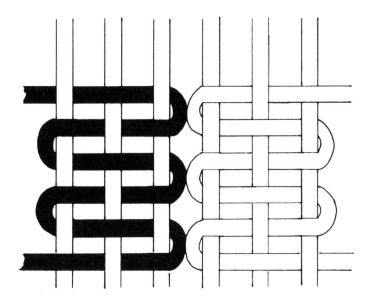

The Sampler. After weaving ½″ of plain weave, weave 1″ in the slit tapestry technique.

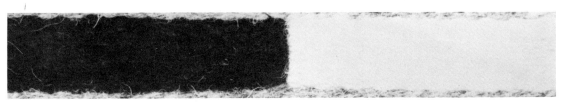

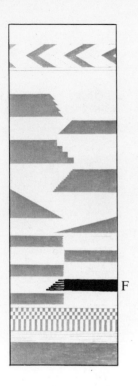

Comb Pattern (F)

The comb pattern, also known as feathering, results in a middle ground between two colors that is rather a mixture of both. It is worked in a manner similar to slit tapestry, but the two colors overlap as shown. The illustration shows feathering done in a regular sequence, but also consider the possibilities of joining and separating the colors in a random manner.

The Sampler. Weave 1″ of the comb pattern in either a regular order, a random order, or both.

INTERLOCKING (G)

This tapestry method is stronger than the slit technique. Basically, the two colors are brought from opposite ends through the shed. They meet and interlock in the space between the two warp ends before the shed is changed and the wefts are brought back to the selvedges. The color areas will be solidly joined together.

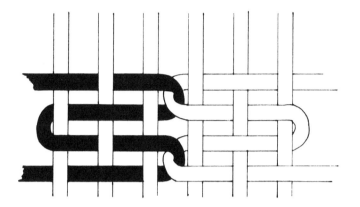

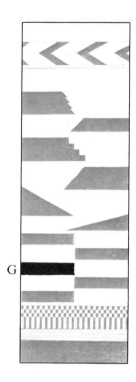

G

The Sampler. Weave 1″ of interlocking tapestry.

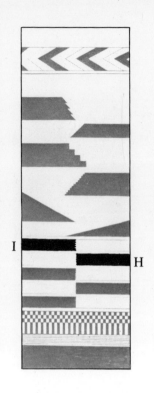

DOVETAILING 1 (H)

With this method, two colors share the same warp end as a pivot point. Color A reaches the predetermined warp end, and color B is woven to the same warp end. Both colors now turn around the same warp end, the shed is changed, and the colors are brought back to the selvedges. This process alternates the two colors where they join around the warp. As you can see, there is a doubly heavy build-up of weft on the joining warp thread, and extra beating is required to make the weft lie flat. The advantage of this method is that it produces the strongest join.

DOVETAILING 2 (I)

Another method of dovetailing produces a different look. Instead of the colors alternating one at a time, one weft thread covers the same area several times before the other color is woven. In the illustration, color B goes around the same warp thread three times before color A takes its turn. The effect is a large, well-defined saw-toothed joining.

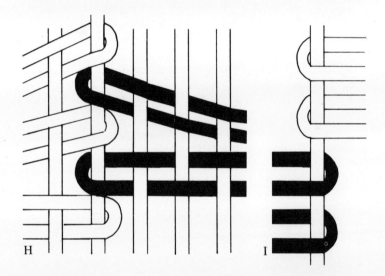

The Sampler. Weave 1″ in each dovetailing method.

ANGLES (J—M)

Angles are simply a variation of the slit tapestry technique. The simplest angle is made by color A meeting color B as in the slit technique, but on every subsequent row, one color advances by one warp end while the other color recedes by one warp end, as shown in the illustration. There are several variations on this simple angle. For an oblique angle, one color advances by two or three warp ends and the other color recedes by the same amount. A slightly stepped obtuse angle is made by catching the same warp end two or more times before receding or advancing. A more defined stepped angle is produced by circling the same warp end five times, then receding by four warp ends. With this last technique, the weft should be interlocked to prevent slits.

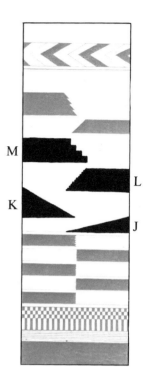

The Sampler. Weave at least 1½″ using each type of angle: simple, oblique, and stepped. Notice that the angles can change depending on how much force is used to beat the weft.

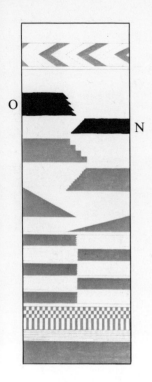

DOVETAILED AND SERRATED ANGLES (N AND O)

The dovetailed technique can also be used to make an angle similar to the simple angle. As shown in the photograph, the angle is made by receding one warp end after each dovetail. The serrated angle is the most visually dynamic angle, but also the most difficult to weave. As shown in the illustration, the weft recedes for several shots and then juts out again before receding further. Unlike the other angles where one area can be built up before another is begun, this technique requires that the colors be worked simultaneously.

The Sampler. Weave at least 1½″ of both the dovetailed angle and the serrated angle.

THE LAZY LINE (P)

The lazy line is a typically Navajo technique used primarily when the width of the weaving is too wide for the shuttle to be easily passed through the shed. Essentially it is a simple angle woven with a solid color of yarn, and it enables the weaver to build up one area of weft before proceding to the next area. Most of the time the lazy line is nearly invisible. Slight variations in the yarn color, however, can give the weaving a richly textured appearance as the line meanders through one area, then another. The lazy line also gives the weaving more elasticity than if the weft had been woven selvedge to selvedge.

P

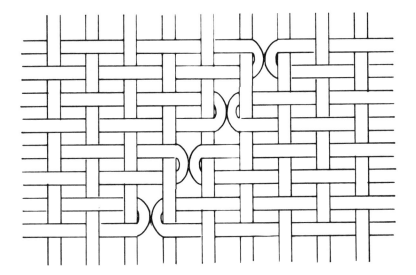

The Sampler. Even though you have already woven this technique in two colors, try at least 1½″ in a solid color to see how the line looks and feels.

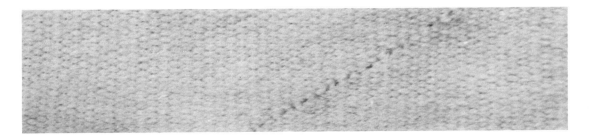

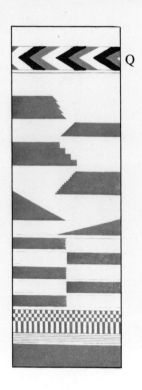

Wedge Weave (Q)

This technique is particularly interesting because the weft, woven diagonally to the warp, builds up to form a wedge. The process evolved in an effort to create a zigzag pattern more easily than with the traditional angle. As you can see in illustration 1, an area normally covered by 11 shots of weft takes only six shots with the wedge weave. The wedge weave has developed into a style having its own distinctive merits, and it works best with many colors. To begin, the weft is wrapped twice around the first warp of the left selvedge. Next it goes over, then under the second warp, then back to the selvedge. In the next shot the weft goes to the third warp strand, and so on until the desired area is built up (2). Colors can be changed as often as desired. When the right-hand selvedge is reached, the process is again repeated, but going from right to left (3). The alternate angles tend to pull the warp slightly from one side to the other, hence the characteristic scalloped edges. Wedge weave is also called pulled warp or lightning design.

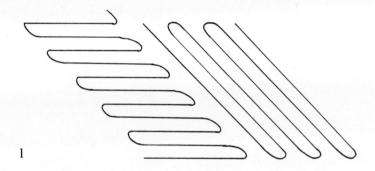

1

The Sampler. Weave 2″ of wedge weave, 1″ in each direction. You should now be about 2″ from the top of your sampler. Finish off with as much plain weave as is necessary (see Chapter 3 for instructions on weaving the last few rows).

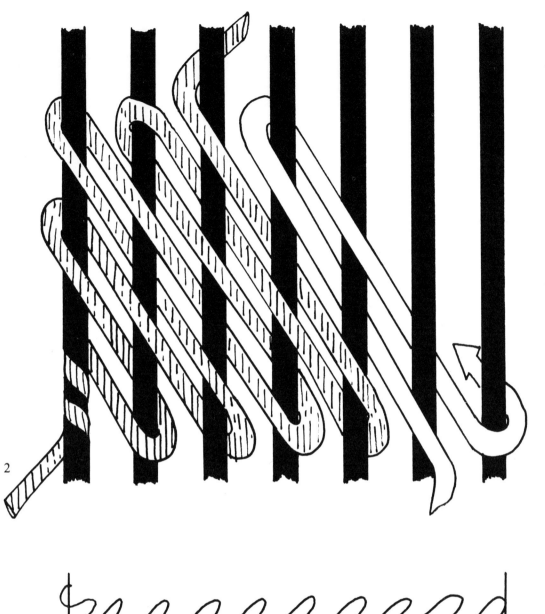

2

3

Figure 12. *Here are the types of patterns that are typical of Navajo rugs.*

Figure 13. *On the right side of this diagram is the simple angle; on the left side is interlocking tapestry.*

WEAVING THE DESIGN

There is no mystery to weaving the design; it is composed of the techniques you have just used on the sampler. An example of some typical patterns is shown in Figure 12. In general, most designs are woven using a combination of techniques, mainly interlocking tapestry combined with the simple angle (Figure 13). The only problems you are likely to encounter are where to begin or end weaving a shape, and which shape to weave first. Figures 14–18 will present both the problems and their solutions.

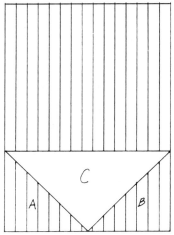

Figure 14. *This is the wrong way to weave a shape. Areas A and B are locked in; the shed is blocked by the woven area (C).*

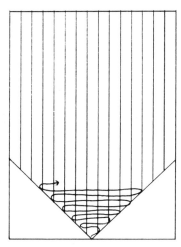

Figure 15. *The right way to weave this shape is to start with the two outside areas, then weave the center portion.*

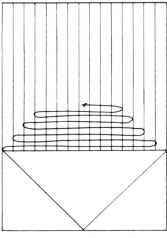

Figure 16. *A second triangle can be woven to form a diamond shape. Since the base of the triangle is the largest area to be woven, it is completed first and the background woven later.*

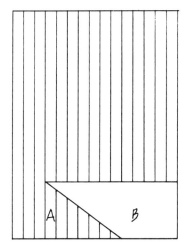

Figure 17. *The same problem occurs with this shape. Area A is blocked in by the woven section (B).*

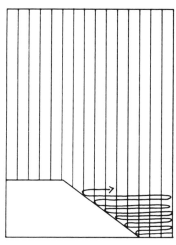

Figure 18. *Here is the correct way to weave this type of shape so none of the sheds get blocked by a woven area.*

THE WHIPPED EDGE

Also known as bound edge and warp twining, the whipped edge is a selvedge reinforcement developed and used almost exclusively by Navajo weavers. It is a twining technique done at the warp selvedges that has its weft counterpart in the twining done around the warp ends at the very beginning of the warp preparation. Just before the actual weaving begins, a length of cord for each selvedge, a little more than twice the length of the warp, is doubled around the bottom crosspiece and warp beam and loosely tied at the top warp beam. Figures 19 and 20 show the twining process in detail.

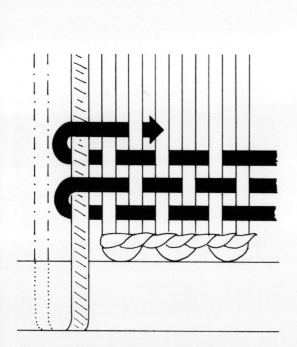

Figure 19. *For the first few weft rows only one edging cord is woven in as the last warp thread on each side.*

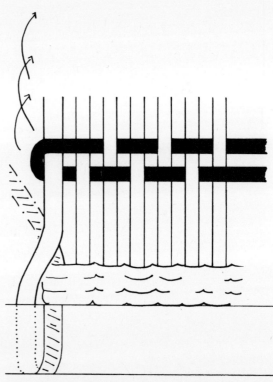

Figure 20. *After a determined interval, the first cord is disregarded and the second woven in for an equal interval.*

FINISHING

The weft twining in a Navajo piece defines the bottom and top selvedges, so except in unusual instances or in some saddle blankets, there is no fringe to deal with. The whipped edge defines the warp selvedges. The tassels at each corner are formed by knotting together the ends of the twinings. Thus, when the piece comes from the loom it is completely finished. Any loose weft ends are clipped at the back, making it indistinguishable from the front.

OTHER TECHNIQUES

My main concern is with those aspects of Navajo weaving that have had the greatest esthetic impact on contemporary weavers: tapestry weaving and the related techniques shown so far throughout this book. There are, however, a few other techniques sometimes used by the Navajos.

Pile Weaves. The Navajo pile fabric is made by weaving long hanks of fleece into the warp between the rows of plain weave or twill. The finished piece looks much like a sheepskin, from which the idea surely originated.

Saddle Blanket *(Above). This luxurious blanket is woven in a pile weave. The Museum of the American Indian, New York. Heye Foundation.*

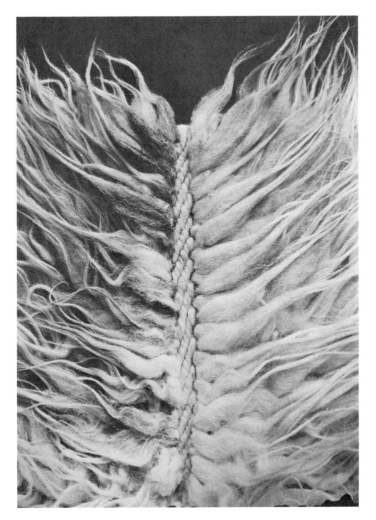

A detail shows the structure of the fabric with six rows of twill between the pile rows.

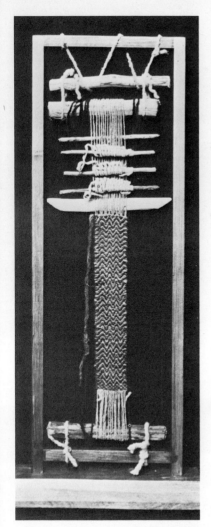

This is a loom set up for weaving a twill pattern. The Museum of the American Indian, New York. Heye Foundation.

Twill. Briefly, here is a description of twill: it is a fabric made with four sheds (a shed stick and three heddle rods). The first heddle rod clasps warp strings 1 and 2 for the first shed. Heddle rod 2 clasps warp strings 2 and 3 for the second shed. Heddle rod 3 clasps warp strings 3 and 4, for the third shed, and the stick shed works warp strings 1 and 4. This heddle and shed stick arrangement is made the length of the warp. In other words, each shed is made by clasping two warp strings and skipping two. With every shot the weft moves over one warp end to the left or right of the one just preceeding it. The effect produced is that of a diagonal rib.

A thick weft yarn will result in a pronounced rib; a thinner yarn will give a more subtle diagonal. Very heavy beating will tend to obscure the twill effect, while beating that is too light will result in a flimsy fabric.

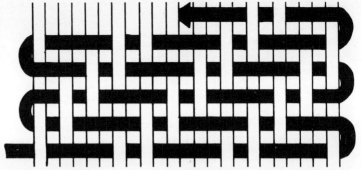

Figure 21. *Here is a diagram showing the structure of the twill weave.*

Double-Weave Blanket in Progress. *Here you can see the loom set up with extra heddle rods for double weave. The Field Museum of Natural History, Chicago.*

Double Weave. This technique is a further development of four-harness weaving. In essence, two complete fabrics are being woven simultaneously, one on the top set of warp threads, the other on the bottom set. The two fabrics are joined because each weft is designed to alternate between the two layers. With this technique, one side of the fabric can be completely different from the other. Today double weave is most often worked on a floor loom, where the harnesses are more easily managed.

Double-Weave Saddle Blanket. *Twill weave in the double-weave technique was used to create this unusual blanket. The Museum of the American Indian, New York. Heye Foundation.*

Grace Henderson Nez *at work on a Ganado rug. The loom is a contemporary variation using 2″ x 6″ wood. The holes in the uprights allow the crosspieces to be secured in any number of places. Photo by Ray Manley.*

LOOM VARIATIONS

Early variations of the Navajo loom frame evolved from environmental conditions and the availability of materials. They include uprights that culminate in a fork so the top crosspiece can rest in the space between the divided limbs, or uprights cut so the crosspiece can be set into them. The latter represents a more sophisticated approach to loom construction. Some possibilities of securing this arrangement are nailing, pegging, and bolting. Of the three, bolting allows the quickest disassembling. A hole about ¼″ to ½″ must be drilled through both pieces of the wood once they are set in place. A bolt is then inserted are secured with a wing nut. With pegging, the most naturally attractive, it is also necessary to drill a hole. Pegs must be sanded to the right size—small enough to fit but large enough to fit snugly. If portability is not important then the pegs can be glued in or the uprights and crosspieces can be nailed together.

LUMBER

Pre-cut lumber makes a beautiful loom frame. It is lightweight, so a small loom is extremely portable. Because the lumber is straight and flat, 90° corners are easily made and braced. There are many variations of the Navajo loom frame that can be made with cut lumber using a minimum of tools and materials. The warping arrangement generally remains the same (variations are discussed in the following chapter), so this chapter will discuss variations for the frame only.

Most commercially available frame and floor looms are made from hardwood (oak, maple, birch, or beech), but a very serviceable loom may be made from soft pine. It is readily available at lumberyards, many home and garden centers, and even art supply shops. While it is difficult to nail seasoned hardwood, that is not a problem with pine—a definite plus for people with a minimum of carpentry expertise or tools. Besides, softwood is cheaper.

The wood purchased at a lumberyard is kiln-dried, which means that it has been seasoned in a large kiln or oven at a low temperature for a long period of time to pull out the moisture. With this type of wood there are unlikely to be cracks, splits, or warping problems on the finished loom that could result from using green wood (wood that has not been seasoned and must go through its drying process slowly).

Make sure you sand down any rough edges or ends of the cut lumber before you begin construction (a rough-grade sandpaper works well for the ends; a medium-grade for the rest of the piece).

Lumber Sizes. Lumber is available in many standard sizes. For your purposes the best sizes are 1″ x 3″, 1″ x 4″, and 2″ x 4″. Originally lumber was cut to the exact dimensions, but today the pieces are not cut as large as their names. For instance, a 2″ x 4″ piece is currently 1½″ x 3½″. A loom frame can be made up to about 3 x 4 feet without need of bracing with 1″ x 3″ lumber; 1″ x 4″ lumber can go as large as 4 x 6 feet. This lumber is generally cut in half lengthwise from 2 x 4's. Used in the construction of wood frame houses, 2 x 4's are able to carry a lot of weight and handle stress. They can be used to make very large looms or extremely durable small ones.

Grades of 1″x3″ Lumber. This wood ranges in quality from the low furring strip to the medium select to high-quality clear pine. Furring strips, which are not kiln-dried, are either rough-cut or planed and are not intended for finish work. Since they are cut from spruce, a tendency to warp is present. Select and clear pine are the two higher grades. They are kiln-dried, contain a minimum of knots, and are less likely to warp.

Grades of 2″ x 4″ Lumber. Grades of 2″ x 4″ lumber range from utility through construction to finishing. Utility grade, usually hemlock, is not recommended because it tends to have too many knots. Redwood or cedar, in finishing grade, is beautiful and smells great, but tends to split when under stress. Your best bet is to use construction grade lumber. White fir is highly recommended since it is strong and non-warping, but beware of spruce in this grade because of its tendency to warp. Lumberyards often offer sales on utility and construction grade lumber, so if you shop with a discerning eye you may find yourself a bargain.

Choosing the Lumber. Ideally you should be able to choose your own lumber. If you are purchasing a small quantity you may have trouble doing so, but at least accompany the attendant into the yard and look over the chosen pieces. Even though you may be purchasing top quality lumber, you should check to see that each piece is straight, fairly clean, has no large splinters, and has a minimum of knots.

A Word About Dowels

As your loom grows to larger than 3 feet wide, you may run into a problem with wooden dowels; they are rarely made larger than 3 feet long. For a larger loom, here are some alternative materials:

Mop and Broom Handles. These are generally at least 3½ feet long, and sometimes even 4 feet long. I save them anyway because they can always be used, even if only as a substitute for smaller dowels.

Shovel Handles. These usually have a diameter of 1½ inches and are generally about 4 feet long.

*Bamboo Rods.*These rods bend easily and have raised growth rings, but they will do in a pinch. If you use one you should plan to spread your warp out to the width of the rod. This minimizes the bowing at the middle that occurs when the tension is concentrated at the center.

Closet Rods. Generally about 2″ in diameter, these sturdy rods are available in lengths up to 6 or 8 feet. I think they are well worth the expense because they allow a loom of considerable size to be made.

Metal Pipe. Not nearly as attractive as wood, pipe is nevertheless cheap, sturdy, and available in many lengths. It can be found inexpensively at junkyards. Aluminum pipe has the advantage of also being lightweight.

HARDWARE AND TOOLS

The major hardware items and tools that you will need for constructing a loom are listed below. Keep in mind that many variations of the loom are possible, and hence there may be many substitutions in materials and hardware. Refer to the list below as a guide rather than as a shopping list.

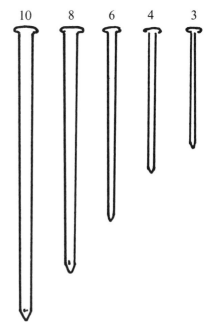

Figure 22. *These are the standard nail sizes shown actual size.*

Nails. Nails should be 1¼″ to 3″ long depending on the size of the wood. Any nails you choose should have a large, flat head. Common nails, numbers 3, 4, 6, 8, and 10, are ideal for most projects. A nail too large for the wood will split it. Actually, your best bet is to take a piece of your lumber into the nail section of the supply center or into a hardware store and ask the attendant about the right nail for your size lumber. You learn a lot that way.

Glue. Some people prefer to glue their frames together and then nail. This helps to make a stronger joint. Elmer's or a wood glue is fine.

Hammer, Handsaw, or Coping Saw. Just about any size hammer will do. Make sure the hand saw is clean and sturdy with 6 to 10 teeth per inch. There are different size blades for coping saws depending on the material to be cut. Pick a medium size one for cutting pine.

Chisel. Use one about ½″ wide for making heddle rod holder.

L or T-square. These are needed for making corners square.

Sandpaper. Rough, medium, and fine paper is needed to make rough edges smooth and gradually work the whole surface down to a silky finish.

Corner Braces. Small corner braces are used for additional support at the corners if needed. They are screwed into the frame with the screws provided in the package. If you use a short screw on softwood you do not have to drill first.

Steel Clamps or Pipe Clamps. These clamps are available in either copper or galvanized steel for a few cents apiece.

"U" Nails or Staples. Used optionally for a latch on the 2″ x 4″ frame, these nails are shaped into a "U" with a point at both ends.

Screws. You will need screws that are 1¼″ to 3″ long depending on the size of the wood. You can screw right into the wood if you are using a small screw, but use a drill if you are using screws over 1″ long.

Screwdriver. It is best to have a long-handled one for better leverage.

Drill. You can use either a hand or mechanical drill.

Bit Brace. This is a drill whose workability lies somewhere between the egg-beater hand drill and the electric one. Its advantage is that it can take bits of a wide diameter.

Drill Bit. This is the part of the drill that does the boring. It should be just a little smaller than the diameter of the screw used.

Rasp. The rasp can be used to scrape off rough edges. Rough sandpaper will work almost as well.

Note: It is necessary to use a drill and screws if you are working with hardwood, but it is optional on most construction with pine. However, if you are inserting bolts, even into pine, you must use the drill.

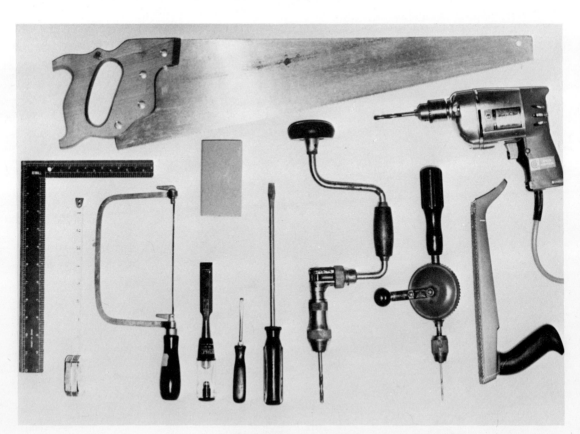

The tools, left to right, include a square, tape measure, coping saw, chisel, sandpaper, screwdrivers, bit brace, hand drill, rasp, electric drill, and a hand saw at the top.

SUBSTITUTING MATERIALS

A number of serviceable loom frames may be made from materials easily purchased or found:

Artists' Canvas Stretchers. Available in any art supply shop, canvas stretchers can be purchased in a variety of lengths. They are made with mitered corners that fit easily together. Very sturdy and convenient, they are more expensive than a do-it-yourself frame, but require no carpentry.

Crates. Since it is really the warp that must be perfectly measured, slight variations in the frame are permissible. Many crates, particularly those that contained large appliances—freezers, stoves, etc.—are braced with good-size furring strip frames. Although the wood is unseasoned (green) when the frame is made, it will have aged somewhat in the interim between making the frame, crating, and finally unpacking the appliance. You might try garden stores, snowmobile centers, or any other place where large machines or appliances are sold.

Additionally, if you up-end a sturdy wooden crate or box and attach dowels to the open side, you will have created a freestanding loom. If you are a dyed-in-the-wool bargain hunter these ideas are for you.

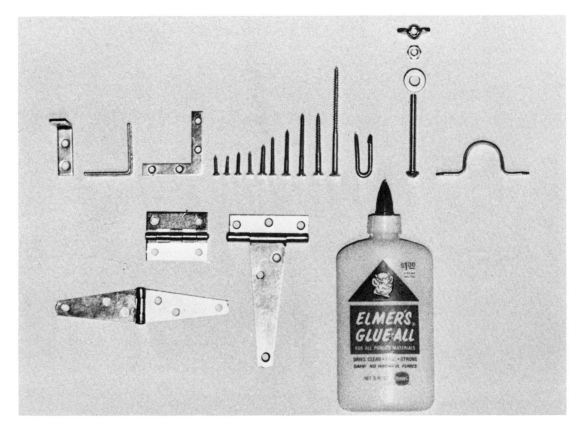

Hardware includes strap, butt, and T-hinges, Elmer's glue, corner braces, screws, a U nail, a bolt with washer, a hexagonal nut and wingnut, and a pipe clamp.

Loom Variation 1

In this first loom variation, two equal-length crosspieces are attached to two equal-length uprights as shown. Use a T-square to make sure that the corners are square (the crosspieces and uprights should be at right angles to each other). The joins can be glued if desired, then nailed together. The five-point nail arrangement shown assures a sturdy frame. The maximum size that you can make this loom varies with the size lumber used. With 1″ x 3″ lumber you can make a loom up to 3 x 4 feet; 1″ x 4″ lumber can make a loom up to 4 x 6 feet. Beyond those dimensions you will find the loom too unstable and too unwieldy.

Materials:
four pieces 1″ x 3″ or 1″ x 4″ pine lumber
twenty #3 common nails
hammer
T-square
sandpaper

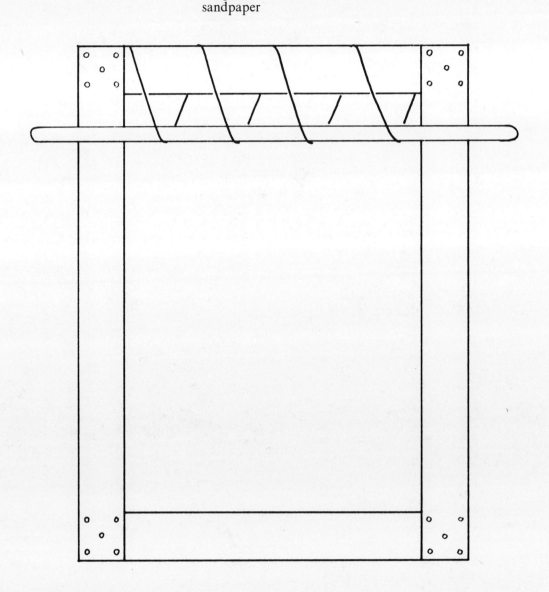

LOOM VARIATION 2

This is the same type of loom as Variation 1, except that the
warp and cloth beams (dowels) are attached to the uprights
with steel clamps. The clamps should be nailed into the proper
position on the uprights.

Materials:
four pieces 1″ x 3″ or 1″ x 4″ pine lumber
twenty #3 common nails
eight nails with large heads for clamps
four steel clamps
hammer
T-square
sandpaper

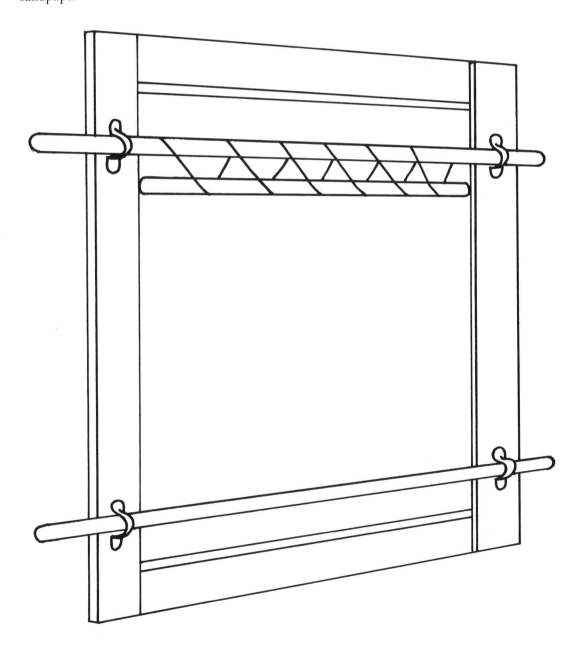

LOOM VARIATION 3

An ingenious folding frame is easily made by cutting a simple frame exactly in half, then reattaching it with strap hinges. This makes the loom extremely portable as it can be folded over to half its size. This particular way of hinging will work for any size loom; the size of the hinges should increase along with the size of the lumber and the dimensions of the loom (1).

To make the loom rigid when unfolded, two lengths of wood are cut and placed centrally under the hinged part of the frame. Next drill two holes through both pieces of wood— (3) on each side of the hinge. This is repeated on the other side of the frame. The braces are then secured with bolts, wing nuts and washers, and the loom is ready to be used.

Materials:
four pieces 1″ x 4″ pine lumber
twenty #4 common nails
two butt, T, or strap hinges and screws
four ¼″ screwhead bolts, 3″ long
eight washers
four wing nuts
saw
hammer
T-square
sandpaper
screwdriver
hand drill
¼″ drill bit

1

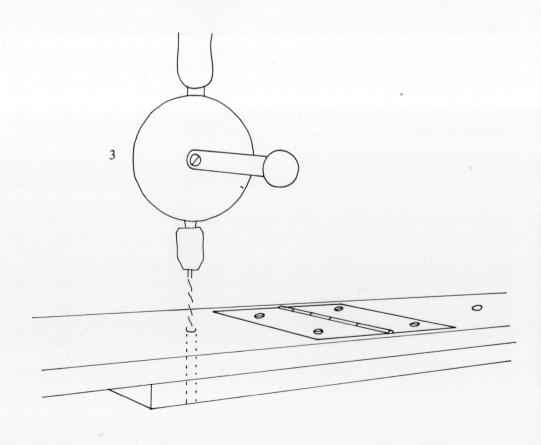

2

3

The loom easily folds in half. Below it is a heddle rod holder that is also easily attached to the frame with bolts and wingnuts.

A detail shows the loom open and secured with a block of wood. This also shows the position of the heddle rod holder.

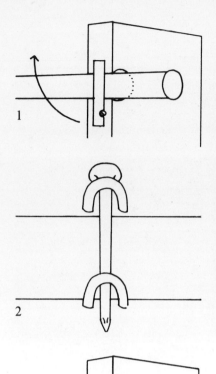

LOOM VARIATION 4

A free-standing 2 x 4 loom frame can be made in several ways. Basically, two crosspieces and two uprights, each equal in length, are attached with butted corners. The illustration (4) shows two ways of joining at the corners: either by countersinking screws (a hole is drilled first, then the screw set in), or with nails and L-shaped angle braces. The larger the loom, the larger the braces should be (for a really large loom, use shelf brackets).

Once the basic frame is complete, there are several ways to attach the top dowel. Holes can be drilled with a hole saw (a device to cut holes for locks in doors), or a small hole can be drilled and then enlarged with a coping saw. The dowel is then simply inserted in the holes. Another method is to cut a C-shape in the side of each upright with a coping saw (1). The dowel is set in and held in place with either a store-bought latch or a latch made from a #10 common nail slipped between two U-nails (2). The dowel can also be held in place with a piece of leather thong or rope as shown (3).

In all versions of the loom, the bottom dowel is attached to the bottom crosspiece by tying it with rope or attaching it to the 2 x 4 with steel clamps.

Materials:
four pieces of 2″ x 4″ lumber
eight 3″ screws, or 8 #10 common nails
four braces and screws
hammer
T-square
coping saw
drill and drill bit
latch or U-nails (optional)

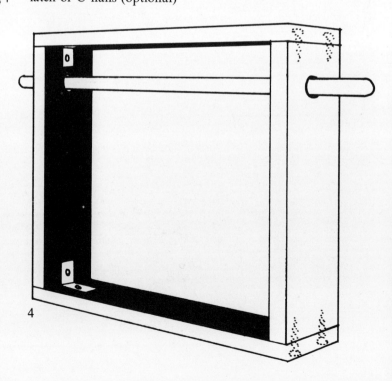

Here is a large free-standing loom with a different type of bottom arrangement.

Loom Variation 5

A permanent floor-to-ceiling loom can be made with 2″ x 6″ lumber. The plan illustrated is sturdy, yet made with a minimum of lumber or equipment. It can be an attractive piece of furniture if well-finished, and when a weaving is in progress it functions visually as an ever-growing piece of two-dimensional art.

The height of the 2″ x 6″ uprights will be the height from floor to ceiling in the room. The width is up to you. One determining factor might be the placement of the 2″ x 2″ supports on each end of the uprights. These supports must be nailed into the ceiling and floor. In a wood frame house, the ceiling will have concealed supports. Tap with a hammer until you hear something solid, then nail your support into that. In many modern apartments, however, the supports are metal and the ceiling is suspended. In that case it is wisest to forego the loom supports, and instead run a 1″ x 6″ crosspiece from one upright to the other. In either case, the bottom supports can be nailed into the floor. You could also make a frame like the 2 x 4 loom, but on a larger scale using 6″ wide lumber and shelf brackets to brace the corners.

When planning the loom, make sure you measure from floor to ceiling on both sides of the proposed loom space because rooms are often just a bit off-level. Then cut your uprights accordingly. Also, take any off-measurement into consideration when planning the crosspiece. Shimming the crosspiece at the longer end with a wooden wedge will keep the crosspieces parallel.

The warp beam of the loom (the top dowel) can be set in by either method discussed in the 2 x 4 loom. The cloth beam can be attached by either of two methods. A dowel the exact length

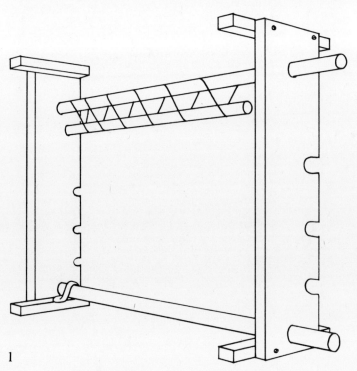

1

of the space between the uprights can be attached to the bottom supports with a metal brace or strap. Screw in the braces rather than nail because the warp beam will be under tension and might pull out the nails. A second possibility is to attach the bottom dowel in the same way as the top beam—through holes made in the uprights.

The C shapes cut in the sides of the uprights are optional, but are a useful way of adjusting the weaving in progress. A second dowel—a substitute cloth beam—must be planned to allow the completed part of the weaving to be stretched around it and then resecured in the cutouts as shown (2).

Illustration 3 shows an alternative upright plan. The uprights are formed with 2″ x 4″ lumber set 2″ apart. Pieces of 1″ x 2″ are attached at the points where the crosspiece will rest. This arrangement gives a more open quality to the loom.

Materials:
two 2″ x 6″ planks of kiln-dried white fir
four 1 foot lengths of 2″ x 2″
two 1″ x 6″ lengths of plank (optional)
twenty #10 common nails
corner braces (optional)
shelf brackets (optional)
saw
hammer
T-square
coping saw
drill
measuring tape
sandpaper
a ladder, and a friend to help

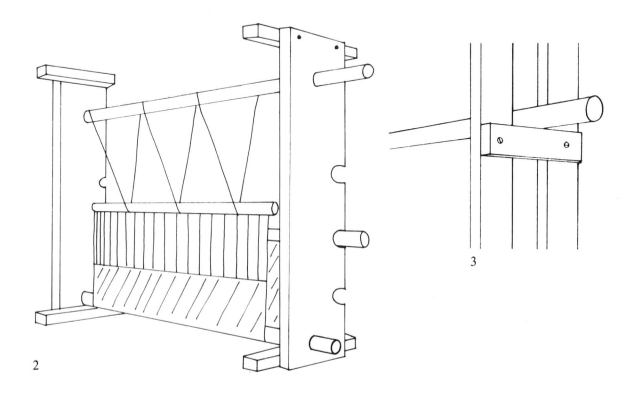

2

3

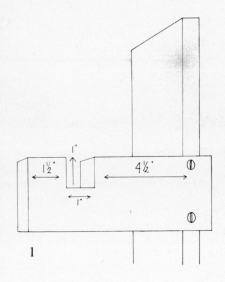

1

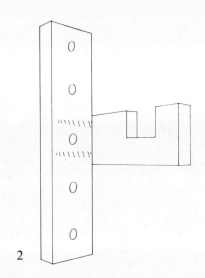

2

Making A Heddle Rod Holder

One of the most difficult aspects of Navajo weaving for non-Navajo weavers is learning to manipulate the pull shed comfortably. This loom variation will show a method whereby the shed stick does not have to be inserted to hold the pull shed open. Instead, when the pull shed is made the heddle rod is pulled out and set to rest in a holder. The shed remains open without effort while the weft is put through. The only catch in this marvelous setup is that there is a point about two-thirds of the way up the weaving when the shed becomes increasingly tiny and it becomes necessary to revert to using the shed stick.

The heddle rod holder is made from 1″ x 3″ or 1″ x 4″ wood. Dimensions should correspond to the size of the loom. When making the holder, the "U" should have square corners and straight sides so the heddle rod will not slide out. Also, if your heddle rod is ½″ in diameter, make the "U" a tiny bit wider than ½″ wide and deep. Cut the sides of the U shape with a coping saw. Then, place a chisel at the bottom of the "U" and pound. This will knock out the little square of wood (2).

Attaching the Holder. The holder should be nailed or screwed directly into the sides of the frame a little less than halfway up. As the weaving is lowered and wound at the cloth beam, the holder will continue to function for about two-thirds of the warp. It is also possible for the holder to be attached with corner braces or screwed into a 1 foot length of 1″ x 3″ or 1″ x 4″. This arrangement is then attached in the same manner as the back support is attached to the folding loom. As a matter of fact, the arrangement is ideal for bracing the folding frame as well (3).

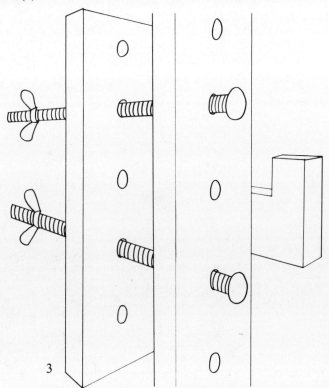

3

A frame loom showing a heddle rod holder.

Making The Loom Stationary

The uprights of the traditional Navajo loom are sunk into the ground—an arrangement that makes the loom quite rigid and strong. Since this method is generally unfeasible for all but the most natural of living conditions (working outdoors or on an indoor earth floor) contemporary weavers must devise other methods of securing the loom. The first consideration is to secure the frame so when it is leaned against a wall for weaving it will not topple forward when the heddle rod is pulled. Another consideration is to make the loom so that it may stand free. This section will provide stand suggestions for all frames except the floor to ceiling loom.

Securing the Sapling Frame. The following method is ideal for securing the sapling or lumber frame loom. First a 1″ x 6″ plank is nailed to a wall. Care must be taken to nail into the concealed upright wall supports rather than the plaster. Leather straps, attached to the plank with nails, hold the loom uprights to the plank and prevent the loom from moving forward. Alternately, straps might be attached directly to the wall of your weaving space. If you must limit the number of holes in the wall, try one leather strap at the center of the top crosspiece. Remember, you can easily replaster nail holes.

A detail of the leather strap.

A sapling loom can be secured to the wall with leather straps nailed into a board on the wall.

STAND FOR THE 1" X 3" OR 1" X 4" FRAMES

You will need four shelf brackets. They come in several sizes; choose a size that will support your frame without being too large for it. On a 2 foot length of wood, screw on two brackets at the center as shown (you will probably have to drill before setting the screws in). Leave just enough space between the brackets for the frame to fit between them. Remember that the frame is two boards thick at the bottom, so you will also need a small block of the same type of wood to fill in the space at the back of the upright above the double-thick crosspiece. Make a second stand for the other side.

In order to bolt the uprights and the additional filler blocks to the shelf bracket stand, it is necessary to drill all the way through the stand and frame—from the holes in the front brackets to the holes in the back brackets. Then attach the frame stand to the frame with bolts and wing nuts.

Materials:
two lengths of 1" x 3" or 1" x 4", each 2 feet long
two 8" lengths of same type of wood
four shelf brackets and screws
four ¼" diameter bolts, 3" long, and wing nuts
eight washers
saw
drill
screwdriver

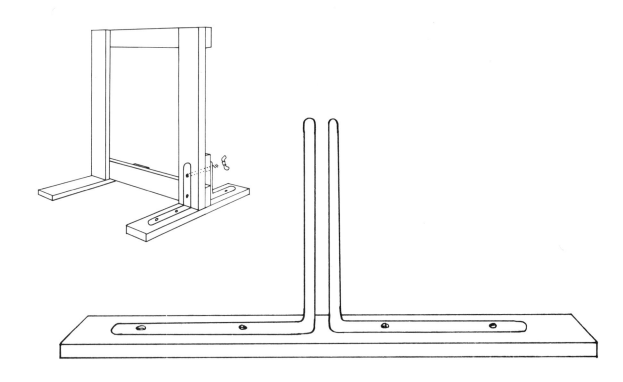

STAND FOR THE 2″ x 4″ FRAME

The 2 x 4 frame may stand on its own if it is small. As it gets larger, however, it may tend to fall forward when the heddle rod is pulled. A stand similar to the one shown here is practical and easy to assemble. Note the curved line of the crosspiece—it is not necessary, but it does cut off the corners that might otherwise be in the way.

Set a 1″ x 4″ crosswise against the upright. Use a drill to make two holes through both the stand and the upright at each side. Two bolts are then inserted on each side and secured with wing nuts. If portability is not a consideration, you could nail or screw the stand directly into the uprights.

Materials:
two lengths of 1″ x 4″, 1 foot long
four ¼″ diameter bolts, 3″ long
eight washers (optional)
four wing nuts
eight nails or screws (optional)
saw
drill
screwdriver
hammer

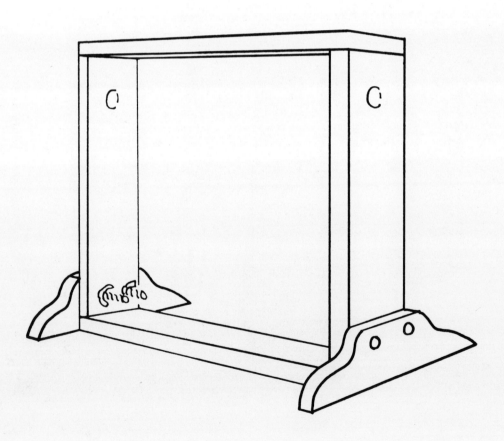

SUBSTITUTIONS FOR THE FORKS AND BATTEN

While none of the implements pictured here has the shape or the weight of the traditional weaving fork, they are nevertheless serviceable since they beat the weft easily and well. The best batten is made from hardwood tapering from top to bottom with a curve at one end, but a very serviceable, if temporary, batten may be made from lattice stripping. Available at any lumberyard, it is a strip of softwood ¼″ to ⅜″ thick by 1½″ to 2½″ wide, and generally about 6 to 8 feet long.

Cut a piece of stripping about 18″ to 27″ long (the only reason for not cutting it longer is that the batten becomes unwieldy). With a coping saw, cut a rounded shape at one end. Sand that end and all sides until the piece is smooth and there are no angles, even at the sides. Varnish at least once, and you have made yourself a batten.

There are some alternatives to weaving forks.

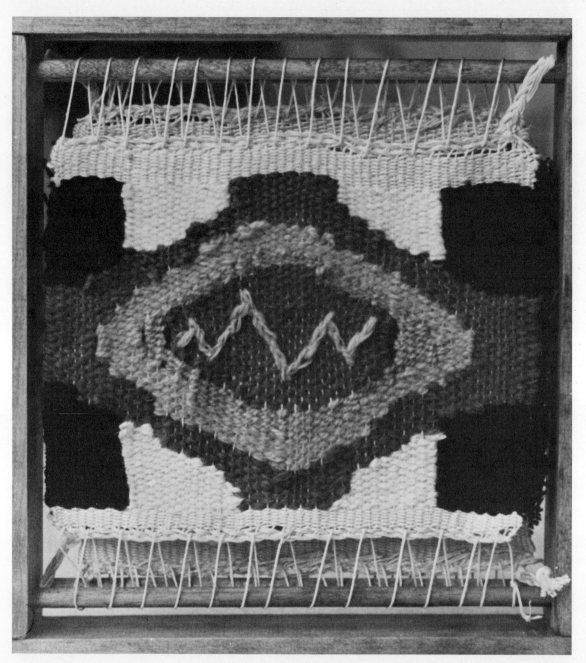

Loom Hanging *by Susan Price. The weaver has ingeniously used a loom-type structure as a means of display.*

FINISHING

In the early stages of building your frame loom you must deal with freshly cut lumber. The ends are rough, and frequently the whole piece is in need of a good sanding. Before any construction begins, it is necessary to smooth rough edges from each of the uprights and crosspieces of the loom as well as from any additional materials. For the cut ends, a rasp or rough sandpaper works well to eliminate the coarseness of the sawn edge. Medium-grade sandpaper works well for the rest of the lumber. (Wrap your sandpaper around a block of wood for easier handling.) Sand back and forth lightly across the grain, since sanding with the grain tends to make marks or grooves in softwood. When the lumber has reached this first stage of finishing you may proceed with your loom construction.

When the frame is finished, the whole piece should be sanded with a medium-grade and then a fine sandpaper to eliminate any rough spots that could catch the yarn or woven fabric. The better the quality of the wood, the easier the job will be.

Staining. Staining the wood is optional, but if you do choose to stain, it is the next step in finishing. Stains are available in a number of wood tones, and add a richness that can only enhance the loom frame. Directions are given on the containers.

Coating. Coating the frame with a natural varnish or synthetic resin is a desirable final step. The coating keeps the wood clean and lends a more finished look to the loom frame. Kiln-dried white fir is the best wood for this project since it is least likely of the softwoods to bubble or buckle under the coating. If your frame is to be permanently assembled, then varnishing after completion will add strength by filling in any spaces in the joints. If the frame is to be folded or disassembled between periods of use, each piece should be varnished separately.

As with stains, follow the directions given on the container. If you plan on giving the frame a second coat, be sure the first one is absolutely dry.

Shuttles and shed sticks made from lattice stripping are also enhanced by finishing. A good sanding with medium to fine sandpaper goes without saying. Coating helps keep the shuttles and shed sticks clean, strengthens them, and helps them to pass through the shed more easily. Coat one side at a time. Make certain the first layer of varnish is thoroughly dried, then sand with fine paper and coat again. Use a good brush and remember that two thin coats are better than one thick, tacky one.

Suede Weaving *by Merle Barnett. Suede strips are attached to the weaving with ghiordes knots.*

WARPS AND YARNS

Since the Navajo method of warping is so ideal, why bother to discuss variations of the procedure? Well, it *is* a long process, and while it may be perfect for those pieces requiring a selvedge on all four sides, it does not encompass such considerations as fringe or the application of a continuous warp. I feel it is beneficial for the modern weaver to be aware of several other methods of warping. I also feel it important to explore the function of the warp other than as a hidden weft support for tapestry weaving, since the different types of weaves often dictate how the loom is to be warped.

The Warp

Regardless of how the warp is strung, the warp itself may be utilized in a number of ways. First, as in tapestry, the warp may be completely covered. There are usually 6 to 10 warp ends per inch, and the weave is called *weft face*, since it is only the weft that shows.

Second, the weave may be *balanced*, which means that warp and weft interact equally. Most fabric is woven this way; if there are 15 epi in the warp there are 15 shots per inch in the weft. Naturally the number of threads in the warp and weft varies with the thickness of the yarn used and the density or openness of the weave.

Third, the warp threads can be set so close together that the weft thread is invisible. This is called *warp face*, and it is the opposite of tapestry. It is commonly used in the weaving of belts and sashes, such as inkle belts, when the lengthwise threads must be strong.

Finally, the warp can be *open*, where a great deal of space exists between the warp threads or groups of warp threads. Such fabric is generally used for light curtains, casement cloth, or room dividers. Open weaves are seldom used for wear, since the interaction of warp and weft threads is so slight.

Figure 23. *Balanced weave.*

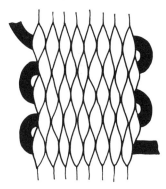

Figure 24. *Warp-faced weave.*

WARPING VARIATIONS

The first deviation from traditional Navajo warping is shown in Figure 25. Although the warp appears similar to the Navajo system, it differs in that the warp is wound directly on to the warp and cloth beams, eliminating both the need for a warping frame and binding the warp on to new dowels. The warp is wound in a figure-eight pattern and uses shed rods to hold the cross. The warp is then twined at the bottom and top. Unlike the Navajo method of twining every other warp, twining here is like that shown in Chapter 8, where each warp end is encircled by two weft threads. The twining is then pushed as close to the warp and cloth beams as possible.

The shed stick is inserted in the top shed, and heddles are made for the pull shed. Weaving begins at the bottom and proceeds to the top. When the piece is completed (and it is not necessary to weave all the way up to the warp beam) the warp and cloth beams are slipped out, leaving a row of loops at the top and bottom of the weaving. Chapter 10, Finishing, will help you find ways of dealing with the loose ends.

Continuous Warp. A continuous warp is another method of warping the loom. It is a system in which the warp is wound

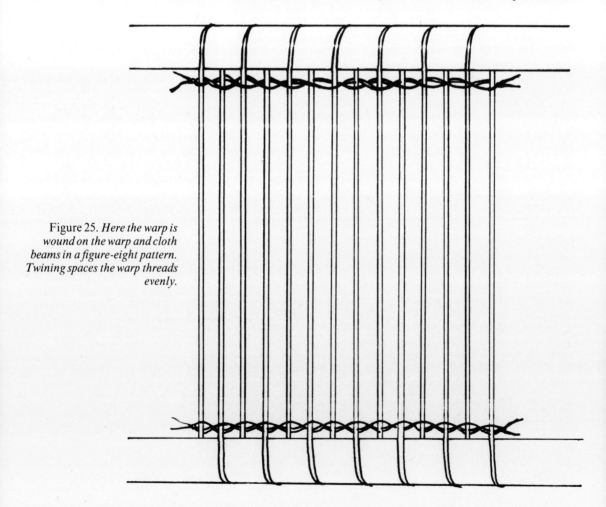

Figure 25. *Here the warp is wound on the warp and cloth beams in a figure-eight pattern. Twining spaces the warp threads evenly.*

around and around the warp and cloth beams rather than in a figure-eight pattern. As you can see from Figure 26, the arrangement of the warp is such that the two sheds are made from the front of the warp only. As the weaving progresses, the whole warp is pushed downward and around the cloth beam to the back. Consequently the warp from the back is moved over the warp beam to the front. Loom Variation 2 in the previous chapter is ideal for a project of this sort.

With an arrangement like this it is necessary to provide some means to let out the warp tension as the weaving progresses. One way is to set a wedge between the clamp and the dowel on each side of the top (Figure 27). As the tension increases, the wedge or peg may be tapped out a bit to allow the dowel to come down slightly. This arrangement is an adaptation of a loom used by the Salish Indians of the Pacific Northwest.

This warping arrangement offers exciting possibilities because it allows a piece to be woven twice the length of the dowels. Notice that the loom shown in the photograph is the folding frame of Chapter 6. The warp is strung continuously with about 6 ends to the inch. The weft is composed of rows of ghiordes knots interspersed with rows of tabby.

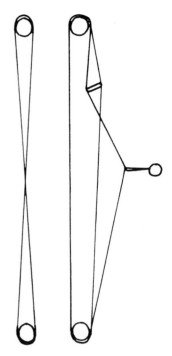

Figure 26. *Here are the sheds made with two types of warping arrangements: figure 8 and continuous.*

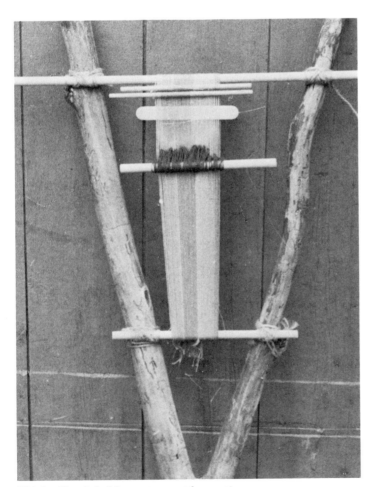

This is a Navajo belt loom strung with a continuous warp.

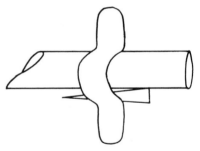

Figure 27. *A wedge of wood set under the dowel is used to adjust the tension of the warp threads.*

Figure 28. *Two nails set in a block of wood serve as a measuring device for making string heddle loops.*

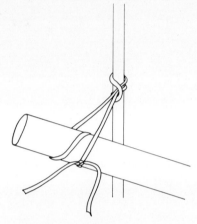

Figure 29. *Use a half-hitch to attach the heddle to the warp thread, then loop the heddle around the dowel as shown.*

The folding frame is a good choice for a continuous warp and individual heddles. Note that the two top dowels are woven between warp threads rather than looped around.

HEDDLE VARIATIONS

One final point in this discussion of variations in warping is an alternative to heddle making. If you have trouble with your traditional heddle arrangement, you might consider using the inkle loom heddle. Unlike the continuous heddle of the Navajos, the inkle loom heddle arrangement is such that each heddle is made individually. The initial process of making the individual heddle loops is lengthy, but the heddles may then be saved for use with another warp.

The correct length for the heddle varies with the diameter of the heddle rod, and a certain amount of experimentation is necessary. There should be 1″ to 1½″ of loop between the warp and the heddle rod. Generally speaking, a 4″ loop is about right for a dowel that has a 1″ diameter.

To make the heddles, first drive two nails (#10 common) into a block of wood the distance apart you have determined your loops should be. The nails should go all the way through the wood; the pointed ends on the other side are then the tops of the posts. Begin the loops by taking a length of string and tying it around the nails. Knot the ends with a simple square knot. Slip the heddle off the posts, and repeat the process as many times as the number of heddles you need. Attach a heddle to each warp that will belong to the pull shed with a half-hitch. Then, working from the right to the left of the warp, loop the heddle once around the dowel. Catch the second heddle in the same manner, then the third, etc. As the heddles are looped on the rod, keep sliding them over to the right to make room for additional heddles. You will then have a heddle arrangement that will not shift or change in size.

YARNS AND FIBERS

Yarn is the most common material for loom-woven articles. There is a long tradition of weaving with yarn; it is soft, easy to manipulate, and durable. Specialty yarns are an exciting addition to contemporary weaving.

Camel, goat, and horse hair, while a staple in the Middle East, are generally unavailable in small shops in America. Thick and scratchy, in natural animal colors, they are very unlike commercial yarns that are scoured, bleached, and dyed. Silk yarn, lustrous and smooth or nubby and rich in texture, is another exotic item. Used intensively in the Scandinavian countries and in Europe, linen yarn is a smooth, dense material, very much like jute in its roughest form.

Handspinners can create their own yarns from a variety of sources—from dog hair and rabbit fur to thistle down. But a quick trip to the little shop in town may prove to hold some surprises. Variegated yarn offers very exciting possibilities for the tapestry weaver. Used without restraint in many cases, the yarn can also be manipulated to create really original pieces. Bouclé, chenille, or tweed yarns are just waiting to be worked into a richly textured surface. The long-haired yarns, mohair and angora for instance, add yet another textural dimension.

Fibers created for other handwork purposes—embroidery floss, mercerized cotton crochet yarn, even thread and other sewing notions—are readily weavable. Also look at some of the ropes and cords available in hardware stores and improvise.

Synthetic yarns are available in a wide range of colors. Most often they duplicate the textures of natural yarn, but sometimes offer qualities uniquely their own. Rayon and nylon, for instance, are sometimes sleek and shiny. You should feel free to experiment.

Unspun Fibers. There is a wealth of unspun fiber materials from which to choose. Rugs can be woven from wool in its natural state—unspun but washed and/or carded. When well beaten and interspersed with tabby rows of yarn, the woven piece is extremely durable and thick. Cotton is not as durable, but it is worth the experimentation.

There are also materials not often thought of as fibrous. Paper, for instance, can be woven in wide or small strips. Tree bark, particularly birch, and wood shavings are also sources for weavers. Traditional basketry materials can be woven as well.

You might explore the possibilities of animal skins—from old fur garments to leather and suede.

Cloth strips are an almost untapped source in contemporary weaving, yet they were used by Navajos and colonists alike. In the early days, bayeta fabric, new or used, was sometimes cut into strips and woven. Colonial women, too, often fashioned items from bits and pieces of cloths and clothing. Interestingly, pieced quilts have a color sense and geometry similar in style and feeling to some Navajo blankets. Braided and woven rag-rugs are also well-known examples of recycled fabric. Some weavers have new fabric specially cut into various widths for weaving. Felt, a non-woven fabric, is another in the long list of weaveable materials.

Natural Objects. Wood, shells, bone, and feathers are still more possibilities for weaving. Working with metal wire, in a malleable, small diameter, has its origins in the silver and gold threads of the Middle Ages. It has a modern counterpart in non-tarnishing metallic thread made chiefly from aluminum.

Synthetics. There is, as well, a whole range of synthetic materials available—from plastic and vinyl to rayon, nylon, and polyethelyne. Explore the possibilities of tape, tubing, twine, sheets, and bags.

It is especially difficult to manipulate bulky or fragile non-fiber materials on a floor or table loom, since the woven piece must pass over the breast beam and around the cloth beam of the loom. With a frame loom these considerations are not a problem. Since the warp is upright the piece can be woven without being rolled, and materials can be laid in the shed by hand, without beating.

Fleece Rug *by Rae Brown. Carded fleece in various natural shades is used as weft for this rug.*

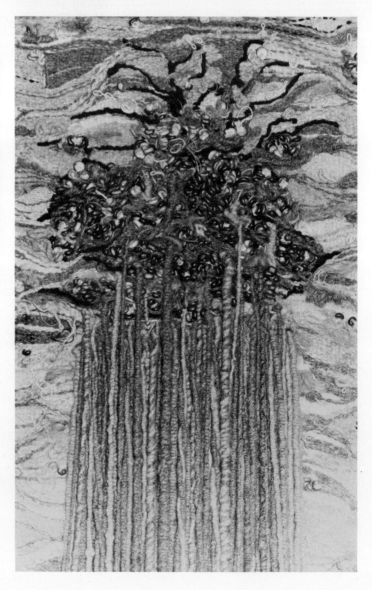

Corn Tapestry *by Sara Hotchkiss. Decorative purple and blue corn has been incorporated into this tapestry.*

CARRYING THE WEFT THROUGH THE SHED

The method for carrying yarn through the shed has been described in two ways thus far—putting the weft in with the hands or wrapped around a stick. Both are Navajo methods. Two alternatives are presented below.

The Butterfly. Weaving with balls of yarn has a disadvantage in that they are bulky and tend to tangle on their journey back and forth through the shed. The butterfly, an ingenious method for weaving small bits of yarn, is shown in Figure 30. Its advantage over small balls of yarn is that it tends not to tangle and, if dropped, does not roll to the other end of the room.

Yarn from a skein or small ball is used. One end starts at the mound of the thumb and goes around it and the little finger in a figure-eight pattern (Figure 30). When there is a good-sized amount of yarn on your fingers—but not so much that you have difficulty keeping it on—the yarn is broken or cut. This loose end is caught by hitching around the center of the butterfly and through itself. The butterfly is then slipped off the fingers. Yarn comes from the center of the butterfly when pulled at the first end.

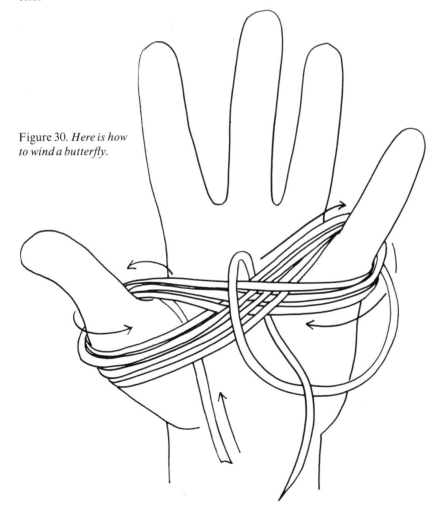

Figure 30. *Here is how to wind a butterfly.*

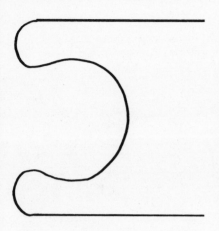

The Flat Shuttle. These are a joy to use, and are ideal for carrying bulky materials through the shed. A simple version, made from pine lattice stripping 1½″ to 2″ wide, is inexpensive, easy to make, and works well.

A U shape (you could trace or copy Figure 31), is cut into each end with a coping saw. These cuts hold the yarn securely and prevent it from falling off. The whole shuttle is sanded, first with medium then with fine sandpaper, so there are no rough spots or angles to catch and break or damage the warp threads. Varnishing the shuttle is optional.

A small length of yarn is held to the shuttle with the thumb while several wraps of yarn are made over it on the shuttle. When the end is secured, the thumb is released, and wrapping the shuttle continues. Avoid overwinding the shuttle; too much yarn will prevent it from passing easily through the shed.

Figure 31. *The diagram above shows a good size to make a shuttle; to the right you can see how to wind the weft yarn.*

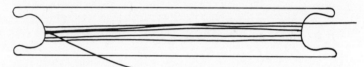

Here is a collection of handmade shuttles.

PROJECT SUGGESTIONS

An interesting project might be to translate traditional designs from their original materials into non-traditional ones (cloth strips to plastic, for example) to see how using new material changes the design visually, or how they dictate changes in technique, finishing, and hanging. Another project might be to weave the materials gathered, picked, plucked, dug, or found on a long walk. The possibilities are endless.

Handbag. *Traditional Navajo motifs are easily worked into contemporary items.*

Sampler *by Margaret Swanson. This ambitious sampler began with simple techniques and worked toward a more individual style.*

OTHER TECHNIQUES

While the bulk of this book is concerned with flat, plain weaving and angular, geometric, tapestry designs, this chapter will introduce some techniques that do not fit that total description. They may nevertheless hold interest for you because they create textures, lines, and shapes not used in traditional Navajo weaving. With the exception of the pile weave, these effects are created from techniques with which you are already familiar.

TWINING

Twining is a very versatile technique in that it does not have to sacrifice its function for decorative purposes. Twining works as a warp spacer and, in Navajo weaving, as a selvedge strengthener.

As a decorative technique, twining has more pronounced texture and is thicker than plain weave, since two threads encircle each warp at each row. In two-color twining, two strands of one color are exchanged for one strand each of two colors (Figure 32).

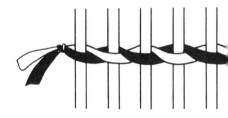

Figure 32. *Two-color twining.*

Multicolor twining, though essentially the same technique, is a bit more complex. Three or more colors are knotted together with an overhand knot. The first twining thread is placed in front of the first warp; the second thread is placed behind the first warp, between it and the second; and the third thread is placed behind the second warp, between it and the third (Figure 33). Additional threads follow that order.

Twining begins when the first twining thread goes from the front of the first warp, behind the next two, and rests between the third and fourth warps. Twining thread 2 covers the second warp thread, goes behind the third and fourth, and comes out between warps four and five. The process continues until the end of the row where the three (or more) strands assume the starting position on the second row and are twined in the opposite direction.

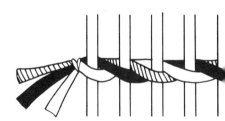

Figure 33. *Three-color twining.*

TWO COLORS ON ONE SHUTTLE

Weaving with two colors on one shuttle is the same as weaving with only one color; the difference is that the weft, being bicolored, produces a mottled effect.

Two colors are wound around a shuttle at the same time. Unless the effect is to be hit and miss, care is taken to wind the shuttle so that the color on the right stays on the right and the one on the left remains there. As you can see from the diagram, several effects can be obtained from this shuttle arrangement.

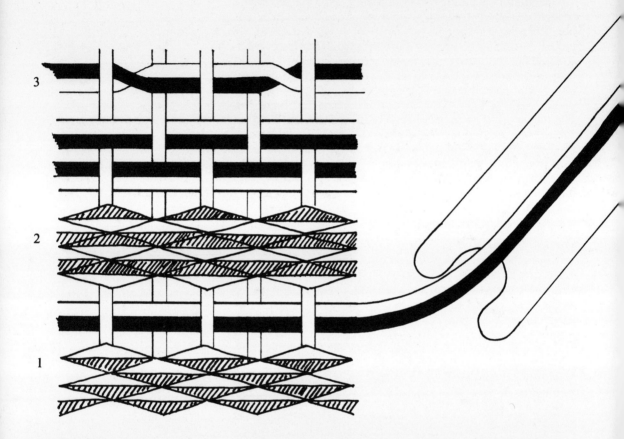

Figure 34. *1) The wefts can be kept in the same position throughout. 2) The weft colors can be alternated with each row. 3) The threads can be twisted at regular intervals to produce a twill effect.*

GHIORDES KNOT

A pile surface is one in which cut or uncut loops fill the surface of a woven piece. Pile techniques have traditionally been used on upright looms throughout the East to Finland and Sweden and to Africa.

The ghiordes knot, pronounced *your-deez*, is one of many that produces a pile surface; it is the one used on most Oriental carpets and Scandinavian ryas. Like twining, it is an ancient weaving technique used primarily with a shedless warp.

The ghiordes is the simplest and strongest of the knots. Manipulated with both hands, two ends of one short length of fiber are wrapped around two adjacent warp ends and then pulled through the space between them (Figure 35). Its strength lies in the fact that a tug on either or both of the free ends of the completed knot will serve to strengthen the knot rather than to pull it out. A row of knots is tied to the warp threads and alternated with one or several rows of plain weave. The technique is ideal for those of you who are interested in subtle color gradations. An additional attraction is that the short lengths of fiber can either be from thrums or small bits of yarn left over from other projects.

The length of the pile may range from about ¼″ to several inches in length—the difference between a plush raised pile and a long shag. The ghiordes knot may also be used to attach lengths of yarn or other materials to the warp.

Ghiordes Knot Tapestry *by Susan Price.*

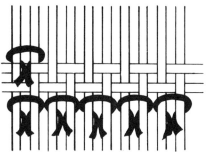

Figure 35. *(Above) Ghiordes knot rows are separated by several rows of plain weave.*

MAKING A CURVED LINE IN WEAVING

The curved line is a versatile and welcome addition to angular geometric tapestry, and it is a necessity in representational tapestry. It is only in very recent pieces of Navajo weaving that the curved line has begun to appear.

The curved line may be made in two ways. Most simply, the curve may be initially created by pressing certain areas of a horizontal weave with a comb or fork so the straight line is made to dip or bend (Figure 36). Further manipulation may accentuate that curved line by pushing up other areas of weft. After the initial break in horizontal weaving is made, additional shots of weft are added by following the line of the curve

Figure 36. *One way to make a curved line is to manipulate the shape of the weft threads.*

or by filling in certain areas. More curved lines may be manipulated as the weaving progresses.

A second way to make a curved line is a method used to weave many circular, polygonal, crescent, elliptical, and amorphous shapes. It is the tapestry technique of the simple angle, except that the shots of weft do not decrease in regular order to produce the angle, but decrease in a more irregular manner in which some warps are skipped entirely while some are encircled two or more times (Figure 37).

In either case, weaving a curved line is a relatively simple matter, while mastering a specific curvilinear shape takes time and patience. The next section will help you understand the circle.

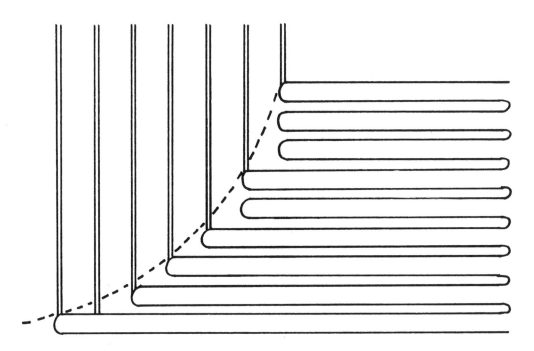

Figure 37. *The edge of a curve can be defined by adjusting the weft rows as shown.*

WEAVING THE CIRCLE

The circle is the most difficult shape to execute on the loom. There are many ways to weave the shape, with the weaver limited only by lack of technical knowledge or imagination. Other shapes, too, can be woven a number of ways. However, it is my feeling that if a weaver can weave good circles in a variety of techniques, then she can weave any shape in any technique.

On the following pages I will show six possible methods for weaving a circle. These general comments will serve as a preface for all of them. First, the circle is essentially the ounding out of an equilateral diamond shape, no matter what the technique employed. The roundness is created by skipping over certain warp threads, particularly at the bottom and top of the circle, while weaving others two or more times toward the sides, as you can see from Figure 38. Elliptical shapes are essentially flattened circles.

Second, the weaving process is greatly aided if the circle can be seen in its entirety during the weaving process. This enables the weaver to essentially "fill-in" the defined area and encourages good, clean circular lines. If an ordinary compass is too small for the circle to be drawn, try an assortment of pot and pan lids, round trays, etc. In a pinch, a fairly accurate compass can be made by attaching a length of string to a pencil. Holding the end of the string in the center of a piece of paper, draw a circle with the attached pencil.

The drawn circle is then traced directly onto the warp strings with a ballpoint pen or fine-point felt pen, or the cartoon (full-scale drawing) can be tacked behind the warp to the frame.

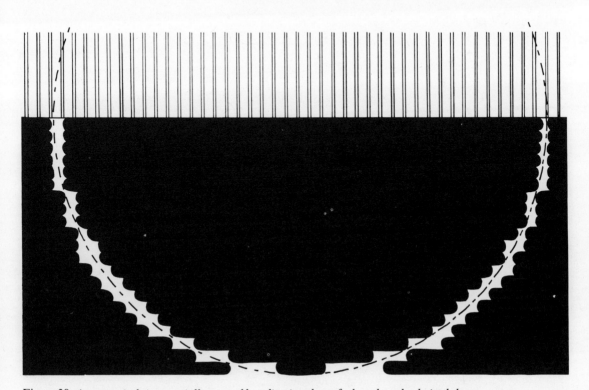

Figure 38. *A woven circle is essentially created by adjusting the weft threads to the desired shape.*

Tapestry Method

The most direct method for weaving the circle is the tapestry technique of the simple angle. As one color decreases another advances over the warp strings. One shuttle defines the background and another the circle. Most likely the shuttles are of different colors, one or more for the background and one for the circle itself.

The order of weaving the parts of the circle is shown in Figure 39. The bottom half of the background is woven first, the bottom half of the circle next, then the top half of the circle, and finally the top half of the background. It is quite unnecessary to use a dovetailing or interlocking technique in most of the circle since the circle threads share warp strings with the background. Joinings can be used, however, toward the sides of the circle where the same warp is frequently woven eight or more times. It is a matter of preference, for the piece can function quite well in most cases with small slits at the sides.

The circle itself may be defined either positively or negatively. When positively defined, as in Figures 40 and 41, the circle is woven while the background does not necessarily have to be. Defined negatively, as in Figure 42, the background of the circle is woven but not the circle itself. A textured yarn would work quite well here.

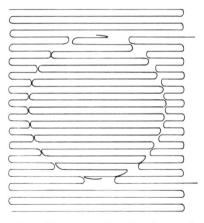

Figure 40. *Both circle and background are woven.*

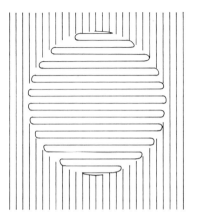

Figure 41. *Only the circle is woven.*

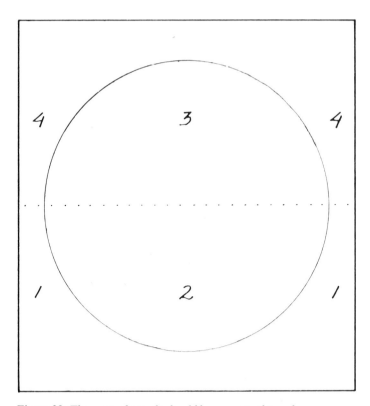

Figure 39. *The parts of a circle should be woven in this order.*

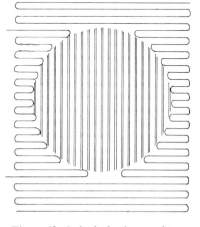

Figure 42. *Only the background is woven for a negatively defined circle.*

Figure 43. *With a doughnut shape, either or both parts can be woven.*

The circle may also be defined both positively and negatively in the same piece, with, for example, the "doughnut" shape (Figure 43). Both the negative space and the surrounding "doughnut" are concentric circles. One is woven, one is not. Such a shape requires more consideration, but is woven along the same principles.

The circle within a circle, the "target" shape, requires more concentration because two positive areas are being woven together, as well as with the background (Figure 44). At least five butterflies of yarn are being manipulated at any given time.

This tapestry technique also lends itself more easily than others to weaving crescent and related shapes. Made by joining the perimeters of two circles at the top and bottom, the crescent presents itself as extremely difficult to weave. Unlike the circle or doughnut shape, where each half is woven the same way, the crescent demands precision in determining which warp threads are woven at each shot. Do not despair, however, for the weaving principle is the same as for other round shapes.

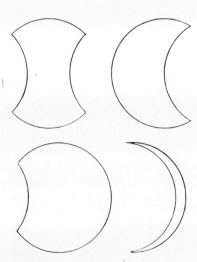

Figure 45. *Crescent shapes require both sides of the shape to be woven differently.*

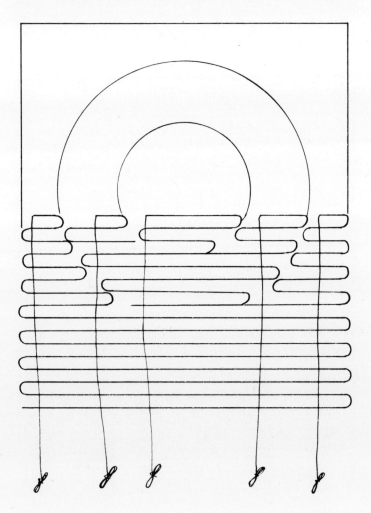

Figure 44. *If all areas are woven, more concentration is needed.*

Slit Tapestry

In the accompanying illustration (Figure 46), each vertical line represents a slit. A circle can be defined by this method even with only one color because the definition relies upon the slits and the subsequent shadows created.

When the bottommost point of the circle is reached, the shuttle or butterfly used to weave the background is then used to weave the middle strip a half dozen to a dozen warps). New butterflies, one on each side of the middle, are added to weave the background until they reach the point where they each weave a strip. As particular strips are completed—the side strips will be completed first, even though begun last—they merge into the background. The remaining yarn is then worked back into the background, as it was before it emerged as a strip at the bottom of the circle.

Bear in mind that the woven piece does not have to be hung in the way it was woven. Hung at a 90° angle, the slits will be seen horizontally.

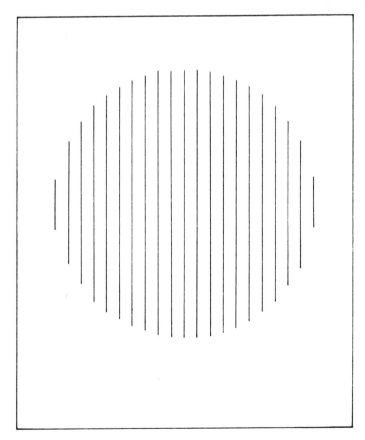

Figure 46. *Each vertical line in this illustration represents a slit that would be left in the weaving.*

DOVETAILING

The circle is defined by alternating stripes of two colors. It is a relatively simple method because only two shuttles or butterflies are used, however the circle is twice as bulky as the areas on either side of it. If the circle is large enough, tension problems could develop because the warp in the circle is being used more than at the sides. An alternative method is suggested next for large projects or for those weavers who desire a more even surface.

Figure 47. *Alternating textures or colors of weft are used for a dovetailed circle.*

FEATHERING

Unlike the circle in Figure 47, this one has no extra bulk in the
middle because an extra shot of weft is thrown in each row—
one white, one black, then white, etc. These extra shots fill in
the space at the sides; I have colored one weft so you can see it
more clearly. This is the same combing technique used in the
sampler in Chapter 5. When woven, both circles look identical
(but you can feel the difference between them).

Figure 48. *Here an extra shot of weft is used in each row to "fill in" the side spaces.*

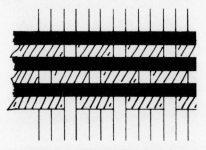

Figure 50. *This detail shows how the second weft floats over the warp threads for the required distance.*

BROCADING

Brocading is another technique used to weave the circle. One yarn is woven selvedge to selvedge throughout the piece as a foundation, while a second, a thicker brocading yarn, appears only in the design area as a float on top of the woven foundation weft. The float yarn covers its designated area and is dropped at the back of the weaving while a shot or shots of foundation weft are thrown. The float yarn is then retreived to be carried back across the warp threads. If the brocading were to be pulled out or caught, as is frequently the case, the structure of the woven piece would not be impaired. Brocading produces a very satiny and rich but delicate circle.

Figure 49. *Brocading uses an extra, thicker weft for the circle motif.*

GHIORDES KNOTS

So far we have been dealing with flat-surfaced circles. In this last method the circle is created by the placement of ghiordes knots in the design area. The thickness of the pile area is determined by the number of shots of plain weave between rows of knots and the number of warp ends per inch.

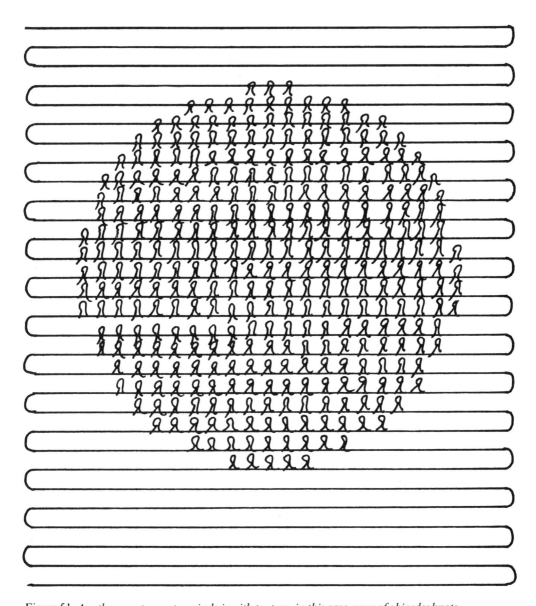

Figure 51. *Another way to create a circle is with texture, in this case rows of ghiordes knots.*

Project Suggestions

Learning new techniques on a small scale is exciting because you not only learn how to execute a particular technique, but also get to see how various techniques work together. I think it is important to be familiar with many techniques on a working basis—then there is no question on a big project as to which technique is the right one for the piece. I suggest you set up a small sampler, perhaps 9″ x 12″ with 6 epi, and try some of the project suggestions listed below:

1. Weave a sampler utilizing twining (two-color and/or three-color twining), bicolor wefts, and the ghiordes knot to create a surface that is rich in visual and tactile texture.

2. Create a sampler in which all lines are curvilinear, using both methods for weaving curved lines.

3. Mix some of the techniques from this chapter with some from your Chapter 5 sampler.

Circles. The rounded line is more easily made by having more warp threads to the inch, so I suggest at least 8 epi for the following projects:

1. Weave a circle that is large enough to occupy most of the area in a 9″ x 12″ sampler. Use one technique, but try it in various colors and thicknesses of yarn.

2. Weave a circle of the same size as the first one with a variety of techniques—in striations—so that you can compare and analyze the results in relation to one another.

3. Weave a small hanging in which three circles, arranged to form a pleasing design, are executed in different techniques. You might use this project as a model for a larger piece if weaving circles has caught your fancy.

Circle Sampler *(detail) by Françoise Couvrat-Snodgrass. The three circles are each woven in a different technique.*

Untitled *by Linda Aja. Motifs found in Navajo weaving are used here for a definitely contemporary tapestry.*

SOLVING PROBLEMS

The problems encountered in weaving are virtually the same whether the loom is of the Navajo type or a frame variation, a table or a floor loom. The solutions vary with the looms, but generally any frame loom on which the warp is strung between two fixed points will have the same solution. The problems are of two types: difficulties with the warping process and difficulties with the weaving.

RUNNING OUT OF WARP THREAD

If you have underestimated the amount of warp thread needed for a predetermined width, and you find the warp several inches too narrow, first secure the end of the warp to the nearest dowel with a temporary knot.

Calculate how much more warp you need (the number of ends per inch times the number if inches needed to complete the desired width times the length of the warp). Measure off that much plus a little extra and roll it into a ball.

Check the tension of the unfinished warp to see that it is even. If it is not, adjust the warp before proceeding. When the tension is even, attach your new length of yarn to the old one either at the top or bottom dowel—*never* in the middle—with a weaver's knot. This knot never pulls loose and it allows the ends to be clipped closely. Placing your knot at either the top or bottom minimizes the amount of trouble encountered in weaving around the knot.

Continue warping until you reach the desired width.

old end

new end

Weaver's Knot 1. *Cross the old end over the new end.*

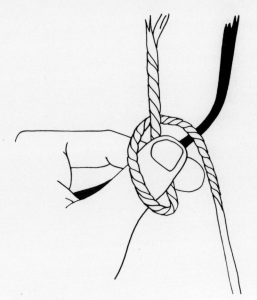

2. *Make a loop with the new end.*

3. *Bring the old end through the loop.*

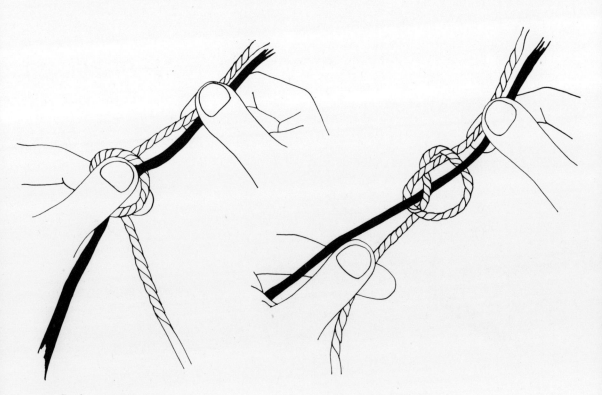

4. *Bring the top strands of the new and old ends together.*

5. *Bring the bottom ends together and pull tight.*

UNEVEN TENSION

Starting to weave with uneven warp tension is like starting a motor journey with a flat tire: expect trouble.

If you run your hand lightly over the completed warp you will feel the places where the tension is tighter or looser than the rest of the warp. Working from the tighter end of the warp, gently tug each strand to the tension of the previous one. You will probably end up with some extra warp thread; just cut it off and resecure the ends.

Lest you think I am overstating the importance of even tensions, the illustrations below show some of the consequences of poor warping. If you go ahead and weave with an uneven warp, those places where the warp is tighter the weft will pack down more securely. The reverse is true with the loose sections of the warp, and the result is a mis-shapen piece of weaving.

If you have not noticed the tension problem until you are well underway in your weaving, working in some extra weft in the loose spots may help somewhat, however your woven piece will generally have the same shape off the loom as on and the extra weft will result in rippled sections. Extensive blocking after the fact may also help rectify the error, but the best solution, obviously, is to deal with the problem at the outset when the correction takes a matter of minutes.

As you become more experienced with warping this will almost cease to be a problem.

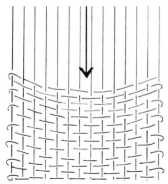

Figure 52. *The warp is tighter in the middle.*

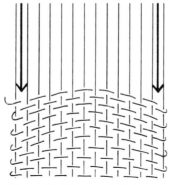

Figure 53. *The warp is tighter at the ends.*

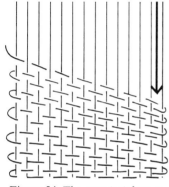

Figure 54. *The warp is tighter at one end.*

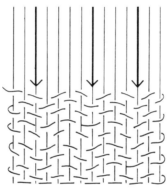

Figure 55. *The warp has alternately loose and tight threads.*

Uneven Spaces between Warp Threads

If, even before you begin to weave, it appears that your warp threads are unevenly spaced, look closely at the twining. A poorly twined edge is at fault. Sometimes one end is twined more tightly than the other, which will cause the warp to take on a shape more rhomboidal than rectangular.

To say that the solution is simply to take out the twining and to do it again with concentration and comparison is misleading because the twining (and the warp) is sewn directly onto dowels E and F. First, you might work with the existing twining to push, pull, and tug the ends into more regular spacing. If that fails, I suggest another row of twining at both the bottom and top—to be pulled out upon completion of the piece—in order to better space your warp. Fortunately it does not take too long to become adept at twining.

Poor Shed

Here is a common weaving problem. By poor shed, I mean either (or both) of two things. Either the shed is too narrow for the weft to be inserted easily, or the shed is uneven, that is, the shed is fine in some places but too large or too small in others.

To make a narrow shed larger, try using a wider shed stick. Also, pull the warp tighter by adjusting rope H or by whatever means is provided to tighten the warp on your particular loom.

With an uneven shed your problem is uneven heddles. Although you may have put them on evenly, the heddles sometimes shift and cause the shed to vary as much as several inches. When this occurs it is very difficult for the batten, or shed stick, to pick up all of the correct threads.

I would suggest some alternate heddle-making methods such as the one discussed in Chapter 7. Each heddle is measured, cut, and tied before it is attached to the warp thread and heddle rod.

Edges Pulling In

A common problem is that your weaving gets substantially narrower as you weave. In the process of laying the weft in the shed you have been pulling the warp increasingly tighter causing the warp ends to pull in. The trick is to catch the error before it reaches the point of no return. First, be conscious of the selvedges; they are less likely to pull in if you turn the edges with care.

You can also hold the weaving out by tying it to the frame. With a crochet hook, pull a piece of string or yarn through the weaving about two warp ends in and then tie it directly to the frame. When you tie one edge be sure to tie the other at the same point lest you pull in only one direction. Do this at one-or two-inch intervals. The second time go in three warp ends, then one, etc. Vary the spot where you secure the string so you do not pull any one warp thread out of place.

Do not pull hard; tug gently. These measures are for a slightly drawn-in piece; there is no way to revive the weaving in Figure 56. Even with concentrated effort the piece would be narrower in the middle than at the ends.

Some weavers stretch a vertical wire with the warp at each selvedge and then weave around it and the last warp thread together so the selvedge stays straight. When the piece is finished, they pull the wire out. (I personally think this is a lazy way out.)

Incidentally, the problem of pulled-in edges is compounded because as the warps are pulled from vertical they become tighter and cause the weft to build up on the sides.

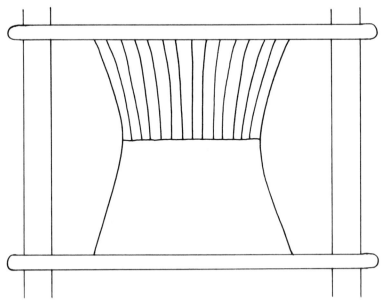

Figure 56. *Here the edges pull in badly because the weft has been pulled too tight.*

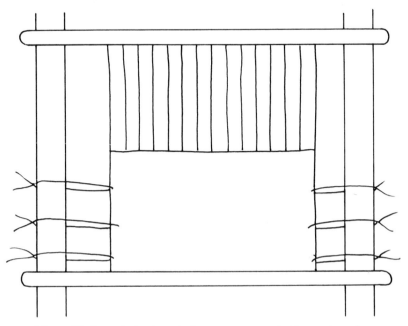

Figure 57. *One solution is to tie the woven area to the frame at regular intervals.*

UNEVEN SELVEDGES

This is the result of carelessness in turning the corner with the weft. The edge is neither sturdy nor pleasing to look at. Concentration and more care in turning the corners will result in better, straighter edges.

STRAIGHTENING A ROW

Your rows may gradually become slanted from uneven beating. The solution is simple. Instead of weaving from selvedge to selvedge, carry the weft only partway across, as in tapestry weaving, to fill in the space made by the slant. If you can see this slant and fill it in before it becomes a major problem, the correction will scarcely be noticeable.

Figure 58. *An uneven selvedge is the result of uneven shots of weft.*

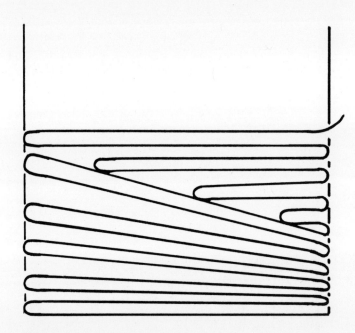

Figure 59. *You can straighten a row by building up extra weft in the desired area.*

BROKEN WARP THREADS

There are several reasons why a warp thread breaks. A snag might do it. Sometimes it is simply that one section of the warp is weaker than the rest. Or, constant shed changing and beating may weaken all the threads and finally cause one or several to break. The worst thing you can do when you have a broken warp thread is to ignore it.

To fix a broken warp thread, the first step is to secure a dressmaker's pin to the woven part and wrap the bottom part of the broken thread around it. With a new length of warp, make a weaver's knot as close to the top of the warp as possible. Secure this new warp thread to the pin, making it as tight or as loose as the rest of the warp. Continue weaving.

When the weaving is completed, the protruding ends are twisted around one another and then pulled into the weaving with a crochet hook.

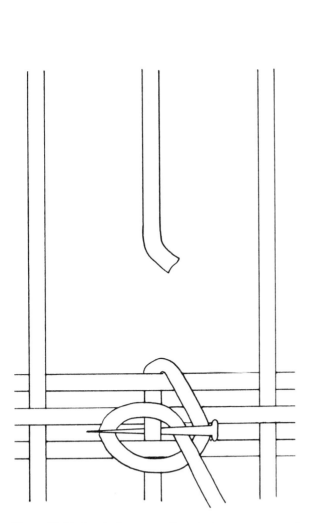

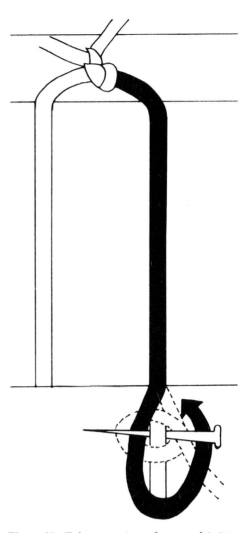

Figure 60. *To fix a broken warp, first pin the woven part and wrap the bottom warp around it.*

Figure 61. *Take a new piece of warp and tie it to the top thread with a weaver's knot. Wrap it around the pin at the bottom and continue weaving. The ends are worked in later.*

WEFT FLOATS

If a weft float appears on the woven surface, it means that you have woven over warp threads that you should have woven under. Care must be taken, particularly with the batten, to pick up only the warp threads of one shed. To rectify the mistake you must pull out the weft to the point of the problem, then reweave. If the mistake has not been discovered until you have woven well past it, forget about it. Once the piece is complete you will probably be the only person who will see it.

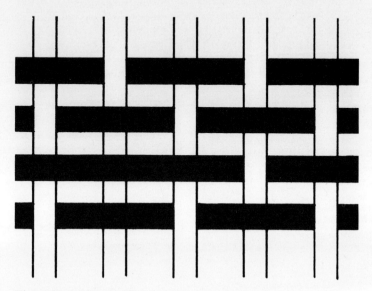

Figure 62. *To fix a weft float, you must unweave to the point of the mistake, then reweave.*

WARP SHOWING THROUGH THE WEFT

There are several reasons that the warp might show through the weft. First, the warp thread can be too thick for the weft. Warp should be thinner and more tightly spun. Second, the weft might be to thick for the warp, so it cannot be beaten down properly. Third, there may be too many ends per inch for the thickness of the weft yarn. (About 6–8 epi with a soft, pliable, medium-thick weft yarn is ideal.)

If both warp and weft conditions are right, here are several other possibilities to consider. First, the warp tension may be too loose. The warp should always be extremely taut. Second, the weft may be pulled too tight, and it will not be able to "fill in" between warp ends. Third, it might be a combination of these two problems. Remember—aim for a tight warp and a relaxed weft.

Finally, the warp may only show through in certain areas. In that case it is a different problem, the opposite of weft floats on the surface of a woven piece. If you have picked up warps from the other shed, or if you have woven under where you should have woven over, warp floats are the result. Again, it is a matter of carelessness in picking up threads with the batten. If you find many warp floats, check to see that your heddles are of an even length and be conscious of the shed-making operations.

One final word about correcting mistakes: no matter how complicated a problem may seem, remember that it probably happened quite simply and therefore can be corrected just as easily. Careful step-by-step work and patience will do it every time.

Bast Fiber Piece *by Joanne Mattera. Here wedge weave combines with plain weave to create a simple but bold hanging.*

FINISHING

The Navajo blanket or rug needs little or no finishing when it comes off the loom save having its ends clipped at the back. There is, however, one optional step sometimes included in traditional Navajo finishing. If a woven piece is not technically perfect—it has uneven selvedges, the top is narrower than the bottom, it pulls in at the middle, or it ripples where extra weft was too tightly packed—then it needs a little help to make it lay flat or hang better. In the old days that piece was buried in wet sand for anywhere from several days to several weeks. When it was dug up it was laid flat on a dry surface and the edges were straightened by stones or stakes applied at the necessary places.

Pressing or Blocking

Today, of course, a multitude of minor sins is covered by a good steam pressing—whether the weaver is a Navajo or not. Rugs must lie flat and wall decorations must hang well. A steam pressing with a hand iron applied to the wrong side of the piece will help it to lay or hang better and will bring up the nap slightly.

Woven clothing, fabric, or blankets should be washed before use to allow the fibers to settle in together and to render the piece soft and drapable. A good washing also removes the grease of natural unscoured fleece or yarn. Fill your tub with enough lukewarm water to cover the piece, then add a little mild soap (not detergent). Plunge the piece in and swish it around. Some weavers have been known to take their shoes off and tramp the piece underfoot while it is soaking in the tub. In a commercial operation, this process is known as "fulling," and it makes the fabric softer and fuller. Do not, however, go to the opposite extreme and put your piece in a washer or dryer. Lay the piece flat to dry. If the edges are not even you can pin or weight them where necessary. Steam press when dry.

Loose Ends

Since a Navajo piece comes from the loom with four selvedges there is no problem with what to do with the edges. But many non-Navajo weavers do not follow this tradition; they twine the warp but do not bind it to a second dowel so the finished piece has loops at each end. Additionally, those of you who have used some of the loom and warping variations shown in this book will have some loose ends to deal with. This section will give you a range of ideas for finishing your woven piece.

In preparing to finish the ends, the most efficient method is to lay the piece flat on a table with the loose ends or loops close to the edge but not dangling over. Weight the woven part with a book or heavy object to prevent the piece from moving.

OVERHAND KNOT

The simplest way to deal with the ends is to take two (or three or more) ends and tie them together with an overhand knot. After the initial row of knots is made (this prevents the weft from raveling) additional knots can be made in any order. For those of you who are familiar with macramé, more complex finishings can be made.

Simple overhand knots can finish the warp threads in a number of ways.

BRAIDING AND WRAPPING

A simple three-strand braid is an ideal way to finish off a piece, particularly a rug, in which a knotted fringe tends to collect dust and wear out too fast. The braid itself can be finished with an overhand knot or with wrapping.

This technique can be used by itself or as a way to end braids or fringes. Wrapping is especially good-looking, functional, and sturdy. To begin, cut a length of yarn about 18″ long. Loop one end into a U shape along the strands as shown, then wrap tightly and evenly.

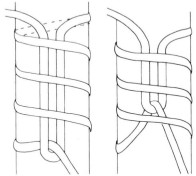

Figure 63 and 64. *To wrap, form an end into a U shape, then wrap around it. When just a bit of the U remains, slip through the wrapping cord. Pull on the free end of the U shape to bring the wrapping cord end under the wrapping. Cut off both cord ends and wrapping is complete.*

The appearance of the three-strand braid can be changed simply by the number of warp threads used in each element.

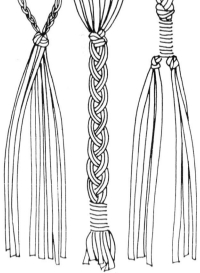

Figure 65. *Wrapping, braiding, and knotting can be combined to make many decorative fringes.*

FOLDED AND HEMMED EDGE

If you would rather have a smooth edge on your weaving, the next two techniques will show you how. To make a hemmed edge, knot the warp ends two at a time with an overhand knot. Clip the ends about ½" from the knots. Then fold the knots under as you fold the woven piece down about an inch. Pin and then hem with a darning needle, using a sturdy but thin yarn.

Some weavers sew a thick piece of twill tape to the knotted edge and then sew the tape to the back of the rug. this eliminates a certain amount of bulk. Avoid using a sewing machine; it looks much nicer to sew by hand, even if it is only on the back.

A good steam pressing is needed to allow the piece to lay or hang flat and without a ridge.

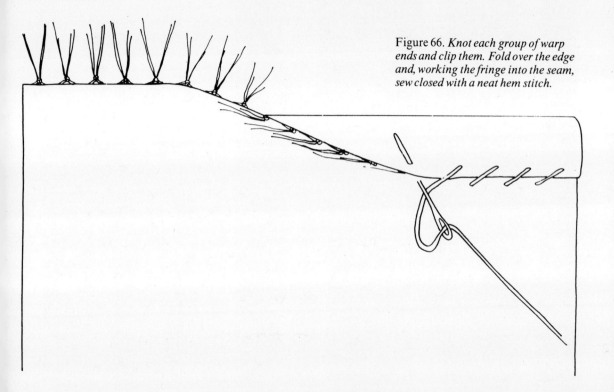

Figure 66. *Knot each group of warp ends and clip them. Fold over the edge and, working the fringe into the seam, sew closed with a neat hem stitch.*

WARP ENDS PULLED INTO THE WEFT

A less bulky method of making a smooth edge is to pull the warp ends back into the woven piece. The loose warp end should be drawn into the space occupied by the adjacent warp end with a small crochet hook. The second end should be drawn into the place that the first end came from. When completed, the edge can be left as is, although the edge is not tremendously strong. It can also be turned and hemmed, or fringe can be added.

ADDING FRINGE

Adding fringe as a design element has its advantages. If you had only short ends before, now you can have fringe as long as you want it. A different color from the warp can be attached, or many colors can be used. The fringe can be knotted, braided, or allowed to hang loose. In the photograph, the fringe is attached to the sides of the piece to complete the design.

Beads, shells, feathers, or any number of interesting non-fiber materials may be added to the fringe to complete or accent a design. Just knot, braid, or otherwise tie them on securely.

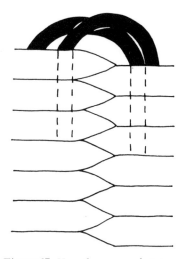

Figure 67. *Here the warp ends are drawn back into the woven fabric with a crochet hook.*

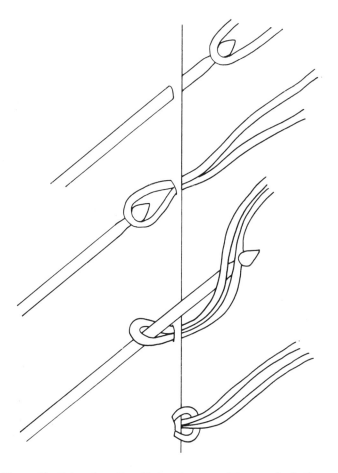

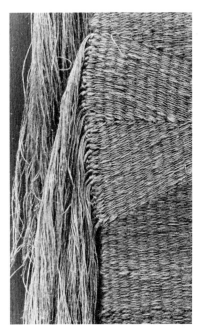

This detail shows fringe added to the side of a woven piece.

Figure 68. *Fringe is easily added as shown, and then can be further knotted or braided.*

WEAVING THE EDGE

Since the woven piece may be coming off the loom with loops, here is an ingenious method of weaving them to form an edging from Peter Collingwood's *The Techniques of Rug Weaving.* Each loop is twisted around successive loops until there are no more loops to be twisted. The longer the loops, the wider the edging. They can either be woven from one end to the other or from the middle out toward each end. In either case the last few loops are tied with an overhand or wrapped knot.

If the loops are long enough to be cut and used singly, or if fringe is added or the piece was woven on a floor loom, Figure 70 shows how single warp ends are woven to form the edging. The knotting at the end (or ends) is done in the same way as with the loops.

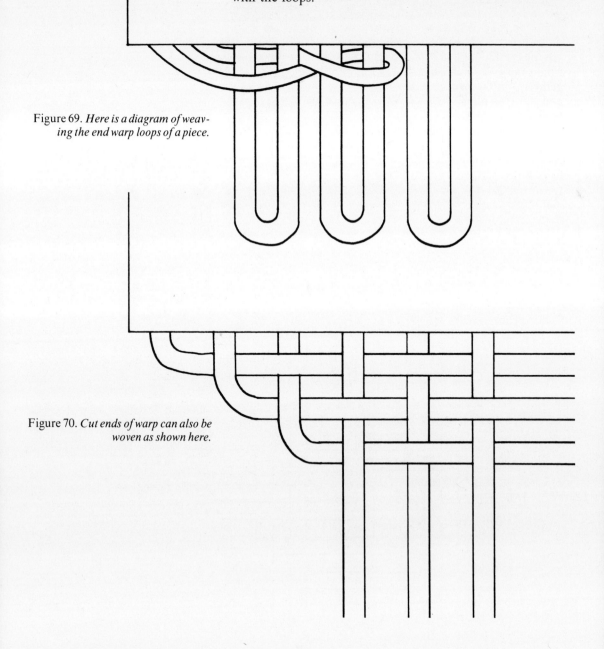

Figure 69. *Here is a diagram of weaving the end warp loops of a piece.*

Figure 70. *Cut ends of warp can also be woven as shown here.*

HANGING

Some woven pieces are not meant to be hung, but to be worn or to cover a floor or bed. In those cases considerations for hanging are unnecessary. With a piece that is designed for a wall decoration, however, the method of hanging must be an integral part of the design. A woven piece that hangs away from a wall or in a window demands the added concern of looking good from both sides.

The most common method of hanging a woven piece is to secure a rod across the top of the weaving. The rod may be wood, metal or plastic, depending on the style of the piece. Plexiglass or metal, particularly brass and stainless steel, work well with contemporary pieces. Wood, the old standby, is appropriate for most woven designs. Most wooden dowels come in three-foot lengths although sometimes a four-foot length is available. If I need a dowel longer than those available, I sometimes purchase half-round molding from a lumberyard and put the two halves together to form a dowel the desired length. I bind the ends with fiber or metal to hold the two halves together. Some weavers use dry branches of interesting shapes, and will even plan a weaving around a nice piece of driftwood, reed, or bamboo.

If you have a piece with an irregular or curved edge you can use plexiglass. When put into an oven and heated (ask the supplier for specific temperatures) the piece can be bent to conform to the shape of the woven piece.

The methods of securing these dowels or hangers are as many and as diverse as the materials. Here are some of the more direct methods:

1. A rod can be woven right into the piece an inch or so down from the top. Yarn is woven above the rod to secure it, then the ends are finished as desired.

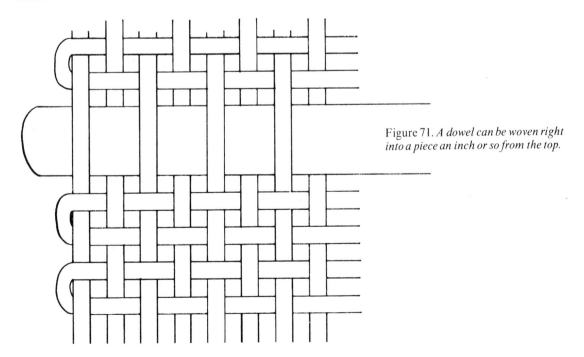

Figure 71. *A dowel can be woven right into a piece an inch or so from the top.*

2. The rod can be attached after the piece is woven with the ends being knotted around it.

3. The top edge of the weaving can be hemmed and a rod inserted in the casing.

4. Sometimes a dowel is used at the bottom of a woven piece. This may be purely decorative, but the rod can also serve as a weight to help the piece to hang better. It may be woven in at the beginning of weaving, attached afterwards, or inserted in a casing. Frequently beads or found objects are attached to keep lightweight pieces down. Heavy fringe will also serve the same purpose.

5. When there has been no provision made for hanging a piece, or when the method of hanging is an afterthought, a good method is to make an open casing on the back of the piece with thin, strong yarn. The casing is made with a crossstitch (Figure 73) and the rod is then inserted. I frequently use this method when I want to display a rug before selling it. When I am finished showing the piece I can pull the stitches out easily; they leave no mark on the rug. However, I find that if the piece is too heavy the stitching and hanging puts a strain on the warp.

6. Another method is to drill holes in a dowel, the diameter and spacing of which depend on the dowel and the number of ends in the piece. The ends, braided or grouped, are pulled through the holes and knotted to secure the piece to the dowel.

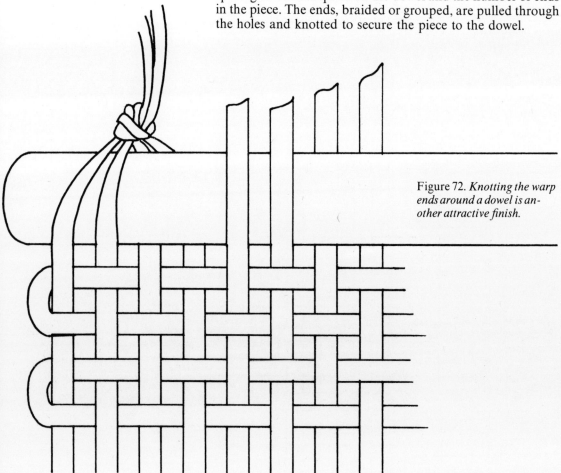

Figure 72. *Knotting the warp ends around a dowel is another attractive finish.*

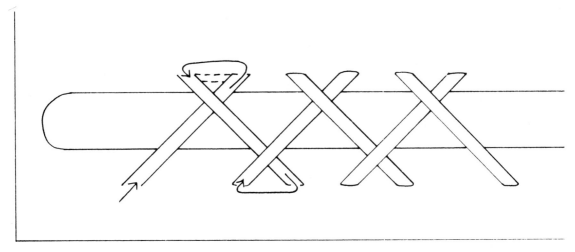

Figure 73. *You can make a yarn casing on the back of a woven piece by crosstitching around a dowel or flat stick.*

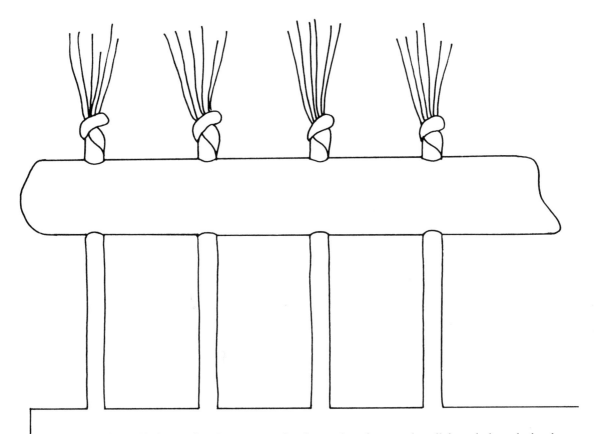

Figure 74. *Drill holes in a dowel to correspond to the number of warp ends, pull the ends through, then knot.*

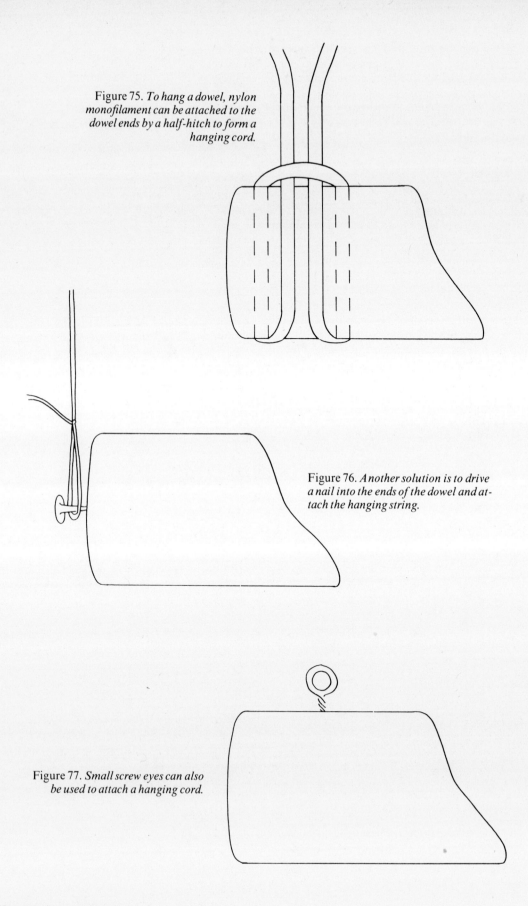

Figure 75. *To hang a dowel, nylon monofilament can be attached to the dowel ends by a half-hitch to form a hanging cord.*

Figure 76. *Another solution is to drive a nail into the ends of the dowel and attach the hanging string.*

Figure 77. *Small screw eyes can also be used to attach a hanging cord.*

7. The piece can be mounted on another surface and then hung. The format is more that of a painting. A neutral linen background is excellent. The weaving should be securely tacked to the background cloth in several places before it is mounted on a board. Avoid putting the piece under glass because the feel of the piece will be lost. Also, natural fibers must be allowed to "breathe."

8. The piece can be stretched and framed. Artists' canvas stretchers come in many sizes and are easily assembled.

9. Finally, the piece can be turned 90° either way or upside down; if a design is good it will appear pleasing at any angle. Actually this concept is not new. Most medieval tapestries were woven so that vertical was sideways on the loom (sometimes for ease of weaving the design, but primarily for strength). In contemporary pieces this means that vertical edges can be rounded and that fringe can come from the side(s).

Once the pieces have provisions for hanging they can be suspended in a number of ways. Nylon monofilament is ideal because it is strong but invisible. Some of the methods for suspending the pieces are shown in Figures 75, 76, and 77.

Untitled *by Christina Wright. This tapestry is an interesting combination of angular lines and soft round figurative forms.*

GLOSSARY

Aniline. Originally coal tar derivitives, but now any dye that is chemically related. The first dye discovered was blue, hence the name *anil* is French for indigo blue.

Balanced Weave. A weave containing equal amounts of warp and weft showing on the surface. The fabric has as many weft shots per inch as there are warp ends.

Batten (beater, shed stick, shed sword, sword). A flat, smooth, sword-shaped piece of hardwood used both to hold open a shed while the weft is inserted and to beat down the weft.

Beat. To apply downward pressure on the weft threads with a batten, fork, or comb.

Butterfuly. A length of yarn wrapped around the fingers and knotted. Frequently used in tapestry weaving to carry the weft.

Carding. The preparation of wool for spinning by straightening the fibers between the teeth of two "cards."

Cards. Paddles with handles at one end and a surface of metal teeth at the other used to card the wool prior to spinning.

Comb (weaving fork). A fork-like instrument, generally hand carved, that is used to push the weft closer to the previous row.

Edging Cord. Plied cords twined at the selvedges of a weaving for strength.

Epi. The number of warp ends per inch.

Figure-Eight. A method of warping around two dowels so a cross is formed in the warp threads to separate the two sheds.

Fleece. The coat of wool that covers a sheep.

Handspun. The single-ply yarn that results from twisting fibers with the help of a spindle.

Heddle. A device whereby warp threads may be separated to form a shed. Usually loops attach the threads to a heddle rod.

Heddle Rod. A length of dowel used with the heddles to create a shed.

Lanolin. The processed result of the grease found in sheep's wool, used as a skin softener commercially.

Laying-in. The process of putting in the weft thread.

Loom. In this book, a rectangular frame inside which the warp can be stretched for weaving.

Mordant. Chemicals used in natural dyeing to permanently set the colors.

Pick. One row or shot of weaving.

Plain Weave. The simplest form of weaving. The weft is put through the shed between alternating warp strings.

Plying. Twisting two yarns around one another to form a stronger cord.

Pull Shed. The shed made by pulling out the heddle rod, and hence the warp threads, from the back to the front of the weaving plane.

Selvedge (literally self-edge). The edges (sides) of a woven piece. A Navajo weaving is often constructed so it has selvedges on all four sides.

Shaft. The long, dowel-like part of a drop spindle to which the whorl is attached.

Shed. The space between layers of warp threads.

Shed Rods. The dowels or rods used when warping to hold the sheds (the warp cross).

Shuttle. A device for carrying the weft through the shed.

Spindle. A dowel-like shaft attached to a whorl used for spinning yarn.

Staple. A lock of fleece that is judged according to length, waviness, fineness, color, and strength.

Stick Shed. The shed formed by placing the batten in the space made by the shed rod.

Tabby. Plain weave, generally balanced so there is an equal amount of warp and weft.

Tapestry. Plain weave in which the weft completely covers the warp. Generally two or more colors are used as weft on each row.

Tension. The degree of tautness put on the warp threads.

Twill. A weave that creates a diagonal rib on the surface of the weaving.

Twining. A doubled weft is twined around each warp thread as a selvedge strengthener and warp spacer.

Warp. The vertical threads stretched inside the loom frame.

Warp Faced. A type of plain weave where only the warp threads are visible on the woven surface.

Weaver's Knot. A simple knot used by weavers because threads may be clipped close to the knot without its coming apart.

Weft. The yarn that is woven over and under the warp threads.

Weft Faced. A type of plain weave in which only the weft threads are visible on the woven surface.

Whorl. The round wood or sandstone weight attached at the bottom of the spindle shaft.

SUPPLIERS LIST

FRAME LOOMS AND WEAVING SUPPLIES

Casa De Las Tejedoras
1619 East Edinger
Santa Ana, Californa 92705

Gilmore Looms
1032 N. Broadway Ave.
Stockton, California 95205

Good Karma Looms
Rd. 1
Park View Terrace
Chadron, Nebraska 69337

Greenmont Yarns and Looms
Troy-Bennington Road
Bennington, Vermont

LeClerc Loom Corp.
Dept. N.H.
Box 491
Plattsburgh, New York 12901

Living Designs
313 South Murphy Ave.
Sunnyvale, California 94086

Lily Mills Co.
Shelby, North Carolina 28150

Paternayan Bros., Inc.
312 E. 95th St.
New York, New York

Schacht Spindle Co.
646 Pleasant St.
Boulder, Colorado

School Products, Inc.
312 E. 23rd St.
New York, New York 10010

Some Place
2990 Adeline St.
Berkeley, California 94703

NATURAL DYEING SUPPLIES

Earth Guild, Inc.
149 Putnam Avenue
Cambridge, Massachusetts

Straw Into Gold
5550 S. College Ave.
Oakland, California 94618

Wide World of Herbs
11 St. Catherine East
Montreal, Quebec, Canada

YARNS

Bartlett Yarns
Harmony, Maine 04942

Briggs and Little's Woolen Mills
York Mills
Harvey Station
New Brunswick, Canada

Creative Handweavers
Box 26480
Los Angeles, California 90026

Custom Handweavers
Allied Arts Guild
Arbor Road at Creek Drive
Menlo Park, California 94025

The Earth Guild
Cambridge, Massachusetts 02114

Fort Crailo Yarn Co.
2 Green St.
Rensselaer, New York 12144

Greenmont Yarns and Looms
Bennington, Vermont 05201

Harrisville Designs
Harrisville, New Hampshire 03450

Lundgren Inc.
540 W. Main St.
Northboro, Massachusetts 01532

The Pendleton Shop
Box 233, Jordan Road
Sedona, Arizona 86336

Roughspun
1545 Addison
Berkeley, California 94703

Tahki Imports
336 West End Avenue
New York, New York 10023

Tinkler and Co.
Norristown, Pennsylvania 19400

The Yarn Depot
545 Sutter St.
San Francisco, California 94102

FOR BRITISH READERS

FRAME LOOMS

Dryad Ltd.
Northgates
Leicester LEI 4QR

Harris Looms Ltd.
North Grove Road
Hawkhurst, Kent

DYES

Comak Chemicals Ltd.
11 Moon Street
London N1

Matheson Dyes and Chemicals
Marcon Place
Hackney, London E8

YARNS

Craftsman Mark Ltd.
Trefnant
Denbigh LL1B SUD, North Wales

T.M. Hunter
Brora, Scotland

J. Hyslop, Bathgate & Co.
Galashiels, Scotland

Multiple Fabric Co.
Dudley Hill
Bradford BD4

Texere Yarns
9 Peckover Street
Bradford BD1 5BD

The Weavers Shop
Wilton Royal Carpet Factory
Wilton, Wilts. SP2 OAY

BIBLIOGRAPHY

NAVAJO WEAVING

Amsden, Charles Avery. *Navajo Weaving: Technic and History*. Glorieta, New Mexico: The Rio Grand Press, 1934.

Bennett, Noel, and Tiana Bighorse. *Working with the Wool*. Flagstaff, Arizona: Northland Press, 1971.

James, George Wharton. *Indian Blankets and their Makers*. Chicago, Illinois: A.C. McClurg and Co., 1914.

Kahlenberg, Mary Hunt, and Anthony Berlant. *The Navajo Blanket*. Los Angeles County Museum of Art: Praeger Publishers, Inc., 1972.

Kent, Kate Peck. *The Story of Navajo Weaving*. Phoenix, Arizona: Heard Museum of Anthropology and Primitive Art, 1961.

Pendleton, Mary. *Navajo and Hopi Weaving Techniques*. New York: MacMillan Pub. Co., 1974. London: Studio Vista, 1974.

Reichard, Gladys A. *Navajo Shepherd and Weaver*. New York: J.J. Augustin, 1936.

———*Weaving a Navajo Blanket*. New York: Dover Publications, 1974

TAPESTRY WEAVING

Beutlich, Tadek. *The Technique of Woven Tapestry*. New York: Watson-Guptill, 1967. London: Batsford.

Depas, Spencer. *Macrame, Weaving and Tapestry*. New York: MacMillan.

GENERAL INFORMATION

Birrell, Virla. *The Textile Arts*. New York: Harper and Row, 1959.

Collingwood, Peter. *The Techniques of Rug Weaving*. New York: Watson-Guptill, 1968. London: Faber and Faber.

Constantine, Mildred, and Jack Lenor Larsen. *Beyond Craft: The Art Fabric*. New York: Van Nostrand Rienhold, 1973.

Cook, Bonny. *Weaving with Antique Fur*. Port Ludlow, Washington: Print Shop, 1971.

Emery, Irene. *The Primary Structure of Fabrics*. Washington, D.C.: The Textile Museum.

Regensteiner, Else. *The Art of Weaving*. New York: Van-Nostrand Rienhold. London: Studio Vista.

Sober Marion. *How to Make 8 Braids*. Plymouth, Michigan: Marion Sober (available from the author, Box 294, Plymouth, Mich. 48170).

Wells, Oliver N. *Salish Weaving*. Sardis, B.C.: Oliver N. Wells, 1969.

Wilson Jean. *The Pile Weaves*. New York: Van Nostrand-Rienhold. London: Studio Vista.

Znamierowski, Nell. *Step-by-Step Weaving*. New York: Golden Press. London: Pan.

LOOMS

Hoffman, Marta. *The Warp-Weighted Loom*. Oslo, Norway: University Press.

Roth, H. Ling. *Studies in Primitive Looms*. Halifax, England: The Bankfield Museum.

SPINNING

Davenport, Elsie. *Your Handspinning*. Big Sur, California: Craft and Hobby Book Service.

Fannin, Allen. *Handspinning*. New York: Van-Nostrand-Rienhold, 1970.

DYEING

Bolton, Eileen. *Lichens for Vegetable Dyeing*. London: Studio Vista.

Lesch, Alma. *Vegetable Dyeing*. New York: Watson-Guptill, 1970.

Weigle, Palmy. *Ancient Dyes for Modern Weavers*. New York: Watson-Guptill, 1974.

PAMPHLETS

Bryan, N.G. *Navajo Native Dyes*. Washington, D.C.: U.S. Office of Indian Affairs.

Douglas, Frederic H. *Navajo Wearing Blankets*. Denver, Colorado: Dept. of Indian Art, Dever Art Museum.

Dutton, Bertha. *Navaho Weaving Today*. Santa Fe, New Mexico: Museum of New Mexico Press 1961.

Mattera, Joanne. *How to Make the Navajo Loom and its Variations*. Shushan, New York: Joanne Mattera, 1973.

Mera, H.P. *Navajo Textile Arts*. Santa Fe, New Mexico: Laboratory of Anthropology.

PERIODICALS

Arizona Highways. 2039 West Lewis Avenue, Phoenix, Arizona 85009.

Crafts. Crafts Advisory Committee, 28 Haymarket, London SW1Y 4Su, England.

Craft Horizons. American Crafts Council, 44 West 53rd St., New York, New York 10019.

Creative Crafts. Pitman Publishing, 39 Parker St., London WC2B5PB.

Shuttle, Spindle and Dyepot. 998 Farmington Ave., West Hartford, Connecticut 06117.

INDEX

Alternating blocks, weaving, 66
Angles, weaving, 71, 72
Aniline dyes, 20

Banded blankets, 18
Batten, 53; substitutions for, 101
Bayeta cloth 33–35
Bayeta serape, 14, 19
Beading, weaving, 65
Blanket, definition, 12
Blocking, 141
Bosque Redondo, 15–16
Braiding, 143
Brocading, 126
Butterfly, making, 111

Carding, 31
Chief's blanket, 14–16
Circle, weaving, 120–127
Color, 33
Comb pattern, weaving, 68
Cotton, 35
Curved line, weaving, 118–119

Darning needle, 53
Design, weaving, 77
Dineh, the, 11
Double-weave, 81
Dovetailing, weaving, 70
Dowels, 84–85
Dyes, natural, 33

Edge, weaving, 146
Eye dazzler blankets, 20

Fleece: carding, 31; washing, 29
Floor-to-ceiling loom, 94–95
Folding loom frame, 90–91
Fringe, adding, 145

Germantown yarn, 20, 35
Ghiordez knot, 117, 127

Hanging finished pieces, 147–151
Hardware for looms, 85–86
Heddle rod, 50
Heddle rod holder, making, 96

Heddles, individual, 108
Hemmed edge, 144
Hopi Indians, 18
Horizontal stripes, weaving, 64

Indigo, 12, 33
Interlocking tapestry, weaving, 69

Lazy line, weaving, 73
Loom frames, finishing, 103
Loom stands, 99–100
Loom variations, 88–103
Lumber, 83–84

Merino sheep, 29
Moki blankets, 18

Navajo blankets, style development, 11–27
Navajo loom: diagram, 38; making, 39–51
Navajo weaving, contemporary, 24–27

Outline style blankets, 21
Overhand knot, 142

Pictorial blankets, 22
Pile weaves, 79
Plain-stripe blankets, 12–13
Poncho, 14
"Pound Rug," 20
Pressing. See Blocking
Pueblo Indians, 11, 13
Pull shed, 55

Rugs, woven, 24

Sampler: diagram, 62–63; weaving, 60–75
Sandpaintings, 23
Sapling frame, securing, 98
Saxony yarn, 20, 35
Shearing, 29
Shed rods, 43
Sheds: fixing, 134; making, 50, 55; too small, 59
Shuttle, 53; making, 112
Slit tapestry, 67
Spindles, 32
Spinning, 32
Stick shed, 55

Tension, fixing, 133
Tools, 85
Twill weave, 80
Twining, 45, 115

Unspun fibers, 109

Warp: continuous, 106–107; definition, 105; frame for, 42
Warping, 43
Warp thread: broken, 137; running out of, 131

Weaver's knot, 131–132
Weaving, adjusting height, 59
Weaving fork, 53; substitutions for, 101
Wedge weave, 74–75
Weft: adding more, 58; floats, 138
Whipped edge, 53–55; diagrams, 78
Woman's dress blankets, 13
Wrapping, 143

Yarn, 35, 109–111; types spun by Navajos, 32
Yei blankets, 23

Diamond Tapestry *by Joanne Mattera.*
Single-ply wool yarn was used in multiple strands
to achieve the color gradations in this piece.

Edited by Jennifer Place
Designed by Bob Fillie
Set in 10 point Times Roman by Publishers Graphics, Inc.

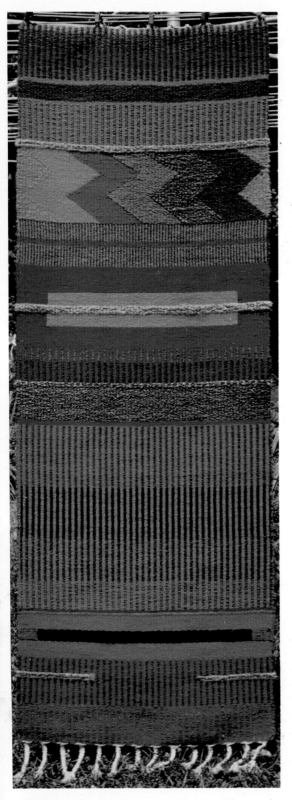

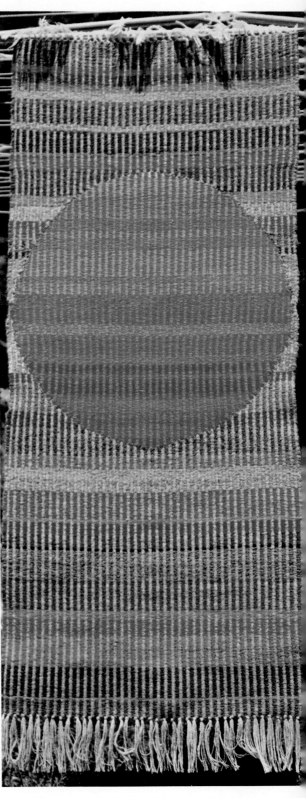

Untitled Hanging *by Joanne Mattera. Elongated beading was used for the subtle stripes in the lower half of this hanging.*

Circle Tapestry II *by Joanne Mattera. This tapestry circle was woven in an elongated beading technique.*